ASPIRE
SUCCEED
PROGRESS

# Matrix

## Computing for 11–14

# Teacher Handbook

**Alison Page**
**Howard Lincoln**
**Diane Levine**

**3**

UNIVERSITY PRESS

Great Clarendon Street, Oxford, OX2 6DP, United Kingdom

Oxford University Press is a department of the University of
Oxford. It furthers the University's objective of excellence in
research, scholarship, and education by publishing worldwide.
Oxford is a registered trade mark of Oxford University Press in the
UK and in certain other countries

British Library Cataloguing in Publication Data
Data available

9780198395591

3 5 7 9 10 8 6 4 2

Paper used in the production of this book is a natural, recyclable
product made from wood grown in sustainable forests.
The manufacturing process conforms to the environmental
regulations of the country of origin.

Printed in Great Britain

**Acknowledgements**
Cover illustration: Koivo at Good Illustration

Although we have made every effort to trace and contact all copyright holders before publication this has not been possible in all
cases. If notified, the publisher will rectify any errors or omissions
at the earliest opportunity.
Links to third party websites are provided by Oxford in good faith
and for information only. Oxford disclaims any responsibility for
the materials contained in any third party website referenced in
this work.

# Contents

# Introduction

The *Matrix* series prepares students for the digital world through a real-life, project-based approach.

This Teacher Handbook accompanies the third Student Book in the *Matrix* series. There are three books in the *Matrix Computing for 11–14* series, *Matrix 1* (Year 7), *Matrix 2* (Year 8) and *Matrix 3* (Year 9). The books combine to meet the Computing Programme of Study (age 11–14) for England. They also combine to meet the Computing at School (CAS) objectives for secondary students. Each chapter will help you to teach a six-week block of lessons in computer science.

## English as an additional language

The *Matrix* series is written clearly for students and teachers with English as an additional language. Writers have used short sentences with a strong focus. They have avoided long sentences and unnecessary words that could get in the way of a reader's understanding.

Lessons identify key words that are central to the topic and may be new to students. These key words are highlighted and defined when they first appear in the lesson. Key words appear again, with their definitions, at the end of the lesson in a Key words box.

This handbook offers a language development section designed to help with any potentially new or useful language associated with that lesson. This is particularly useful when a specific word or phrase may have a different technical meaning from its use in everyday English. This section explains the difference in meanings and encourages you to explore these words with students.

## Structure of each Student Book in the *Matrix* series

All three Student Books have a consistent design and structure. Each book is divided into six chapters.

1  Computational Thinking: Apply logical problem-solving approaches to real-life problems.
2  App Inventor: Create working apps for mobile phones and tablets using a visual programming language.
3  Data and the CPU: Learn the basics of binary maths and the electronics that make a computer processor work.
4  Introducing Python: Use a high-level programming language used by professional programmers.
5  Information Technology: Discover the hardware and software that make up a computer system. Learn to use these safely and responsibly.
6  Creative Communication: Use technology to create a website, conduct research, design and analyse survey data.

Each chapter in the Student Book contains the following.

⤢ **Introductory pages:** The first two chapter pages introduce the topic and show students what they will learn. These pages are designed to help you engage students. They offer ideas for an activity you can do, or discussion you can have, without using a computer. A Word cloud shows all the key words that are defined in each lesson throughout the chapter.

⤢ **Six lessons:** Each four-page lesson in the Student Book starts by highlighting what students will do during that lesson. The lesson is divided into sections that provide knowledge and skills development. A learning activity, an extension activity and a differentiated short test of four or five questions help you check students' understanding. Each lesson is divided into these sections.

   ○ ⌘ **Learn about... :** Sets out the facts students need to know before they complete the exercise and activities that follow.

   ○ ⏻ **How to... :** Guides students through a practical exercise, building their understanding of the lesson topic.

- o ⊕ **Learning activity:** Offers one or more independent activities students can complete once they have finished the earlier sections. These activities are an opportunity for students to reflect on the learning objectives of the lesson.

- o 🌐 **If you have time... :** This extension activity stretches and challenges more-able students.

- o 📄 **Test yourself... :** Four or five short questions give students an opportunity to review what they have learned and make sure they have understood the topic.

- ↗ **Key words:** The key words from each lesson appear in the Word cloud in the chapter's introductory pages. The Word cloud introduces these new words to students. Key words are shown in bold when they are first introduced in the lessons. They are also summarised in a Key words box at the end of most lessons. The key words in the lessons reinforce learning.

- ↗ **Fact:** Many chapters will highlight a fact about the lesson topic to encourage students' interest.

- ↗ **Review:** The end-of-chapter review contains the following.

  - o 📖 **Test questions:** Ten test questions give students an opportunity to reflect on what they have learned.

  - o ✔ **Assessment activities:** There are three levels of differentiated assessment activities—starter, intermediate and extension.

## Structure of each Teacher Handbook in the *Matrix* series

Each Teacher Handbook in the *Matrix* series follows the structure of the corresponding Student Book, offering guidance to plan and deliver the Student Book lessons.

### Introduction

The introduction to this handbook:

- ↗ explains the Student Book and the Teacher Handbook structures
- ↗ highlights the Computing Programme of Study (age 11–14) for England objectives addressed in the Student Books
- ↗ identifies the CAS objectives addressed in the Student Books
- ↗ shows what students will do in the *Matrix 3* Student Book, along with the corresponding curriculum objectives
- ↗ offers details on the programming languages App Inventor and Python, and how to install the software
- ↗ suggests the ways you can differentiate classroom work according to students' ability and English-language experience.

### Two-page chapter introduction

- ↗ **Curriculum coverage:** Lists the Computing Programme of Study (age 11–14) for England objectives and CAS objectives for that chapter.
- ↗ **Preparation:** Explains what you need to do before starting work on the chapter with students.
- ↗ **Learning outcomes:** Show what students will achieve during the chapter.
- ↗ **Introductory pages:** Offer ideas for discussion topics and activities based on the corresponding section in the Student Book.
- ↗ **Six lesson guides:**
  - o **Overview:** Explains what students will do in the chapter.
  - o **Language development:** Highlights words that have a different technical meaning from their everyday English language use, and any other important language issues.
  - o **Before the lesson:** Identifies the preparation you will need to make the lesson a success. This section also highlights the key words from the lesson which you may want to review yourself, ahead of time.

- ○ ⌘ **Learn about... :** Explains how you will lead this part of the lesson and outlines the ideas students must understand before moving on to the next part of the lesson.

- ○ ⏻ **How to... :** Shows how you can guide students through an exercise, which they will complete.

- ○ ⊕ **Learning activity:** Provides model answers to questions or examples of what success looks like if students have correctly completed the activity.

- ○ 🌐 **If you have time... :** Gives examples of what success looks like if students have correctly completed the extension activity.

- ○ 📄 **Test yourself... :** Offers model answers to the four or five short test questions to help you assess students' learning. Where more than one answer is possible, the handbook suggests several possible correct answers. You can set these questions as homework or they can be done in class.

## Review

The end-of-chapter review contains the following.

- ○ 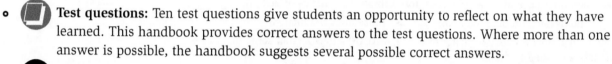 **Test questions:** Ten test questions give students an opportunity to reflect on what they have learned. This handbook provides correct answers to the test questions. Where more than one answer is possible, the handbook suggests several possible correct answers.

- ○ 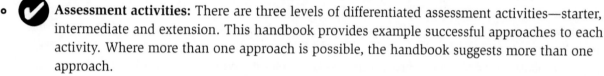 **Assessment activities:** There are three levels of differentiated assessment activities—starter, intermediate and extension. This handbook provides example successful approaches to each activity. Where more than one approach is possible, the handbook suggests more than one approach.

# Meeting the Computing Programme of Study (age 11–14) for England objectives

By age 14, students in England are expected to know, apply and understand the matters, skills and processes specified in the relevant programme of study. The table lists each skill for computing and shows where the *Matrix* series covers each Computing Programme of Study objective.

| Computing Programme of Study for England | Book 1 | Book 2 | Book 3 |
|---|---|---|---|
| Design, use and evaluate computational abstractions that model the state and behaviour of real-world problems and physical systems. | Ch 1 | Ch 1 | Ch 1 |
| Understand several key algorithms that reflect computational thinking. | Ch 1 | Ch 1 | Ch 1 |
| Understand algorithms for sorting and searching. | | Ch 1 | Ch 1 |
| Use two or more programming languages, at least one of which is textual, to solve a variety of computational problems. | | | Ch 1 |
| Use two or more programming languages, at least one of which is textual, to solve a variety of computational problems. | Ch 2, 4 | Ch 2, 4 | Ch 2, 4 |
| Make appropriate use of data structures [for example, lists, tables or arrays]. | | Ch 4 | Ch 4 |
| Design and develop modular programs that use procedures or functions. | | | Ch 2, 4 |
| Understand simple Boolean logic [for example, AND, OR and NOT] and some of its uses in circuits and programming. | | Ch 3, 4 | Ch 3, 4 |
| Understand how numbers can be represented in binary. | Ch 3 | Ch 3 | |
| Carry out simple operations on binary numbers [for example, binary addition, and conversion between binary and decimal]. | Ch 3 | Ch 3 | |
| Understand the hardware and software components that make up computer systems, and how they communicate with one another and with other systems. | Ch 5 | Ch 5 | Ch 5 |
| Understand how instructions are stored and executed within a computer system; understand how data of various types (including text, sounds and pictures) can be represented and manipulated digitally, in the form of binary digits. | | | Ch 3, 5 |
| Undertake creative projects that involve selecting, using, and combining multiple applications, preferably across a range of devices, to achieve challenging goals, including collecting and analysing data and meeting the needs of known users. | Ch 6 | Ch 6 | Ch 6 |
| Create, re-use, revise and re-purpose digital artefacts for a given audience, with attention to trustworthiness, design and usability. | Ch 2, 4, 6 | Ch 2, 4, 6 | Ch 2, 4, 6 |
| Understand a range of ways to use technology safely, respectfully, responsibly and securely, including protecting their online identity and privacy; recognise inappropriate content, contact and conduct, and know how to report concerns. | Ch 5 | Ch 5 | Ch 5 |

# CAS Progression Pathways

Computing At School (CAS) provides guidance for computing teachers and has developed pathway objectives for computing at primary and secondary levels. These are the CAS Progression Pathways objectives covered in the *Matrix* series:

| Purple objectives | Matrix books (M) |
|---|---|
| **Algorithms** | |
| Understands that iteration is the repetition of a process such as a loop. | Ch 1, 4 (M 1, 2, 3) |
| Recognises that different algorithms exist for the same problem. | Ch 1 (M 2, 3) |
| Represents solutions using a structured notation. | Ch 1 (M 1, 2, 3); Ch 4 (M 1) |
| Can identify similarities and differences in situations and can use these to solve problems (pattern recognition). | Ch 1 (M 1, 2, 3) |
| **Programming & Development** | |
| Understands that programming bridges the gap between algorithmic solutions and computers. | Ch 1 (M 1, 2, 3); Ch 2, Ch 4 (M 1) |
| Has practical experience of a high-level textual language, including using standard libraries when programming. | Ch 4 (M 1, 2, 3) |
| Uses a range of operators and expressions e.g. Boolean, and applies them in the context of program control. | Ch 2, 4 (M 1, 2, 3) |
| Selects the appropriate data types. | Ch 2, 4 (M 1, 2, 3) |
| **Data & Data Representation** | |
| Knows that digital computers use binary to represent all data. | Ch 3 (M 1, 2, 3) |
| Understands how bit patterns represent numbers and images. | Ch 3 (M 1, 2, 3) |
| Knows that computers transfer data in binary. | Ch 3 (M 1, 2, 3) |
| Understands the relationship between binary and file size (uncompressed). | Ch 3 (M 2) |
| Defines data types: real numbers and Boolean. | Ch 4 (M 1, 2) |
| **Hardware & Processing** | |
| Recognises and understands the function of the main internal parts of basic computer architecture. | Ch 3 (M 3) |
| Understands the concepts behind the fetch-execute cycle. | Ch 3 (M 3) |
| Knows that there is a range of operating systems and application software for the same hardware. | Ch 5 (M 1) |
| **Communication & Networks** | |
| Understands how search engines rank search results. | Ch 5 (M 2) |
| Understands how to construct static web pages using HTML and CSS. | Ch 6 (M 2) |
| Understands data transmission between digital computers over networks, including the Internet i.e. IP addresses and packet switching. | Ch 5 (M 2) |
| **Information Technology** | |
| Evaluates the appropriateness of digital devices, Internet services and application software to achieve given goals. | Ch 6 (M 1) |
| Recognises ethical issues surrounding the application of information technology beyond school. | Ch 6 (M 3) |
| Designs criteria to critically evaluate the quality of solutions, uses the criteria to identify improvements and can make appropriate refinements to the solution. | Ch 1, 2, 6 (M 1) |
| Red objectives | Matrix books (M) |
| **Algorithms** | |
| Recognises that some problems share the same characteristics and use the same algorithm to solve both. | Ch 1 (M 2) |
| Understands the notion of performance for algorithms and appreciates that some algorithms have different performance characteristics for the same task. | Ch 1 (M 1, 2, 3) |
| **Programming & Development** | |
| Uses nested selection statements. | Ch 2 (M 3); Ch 4 (M 2) |
| Appreciates the need for, and writes, custom functions including use of parameters. | Ch 2, 4 (M 3) |
| Knows the difference between, and uses appropriately, procedures and functions. | Ch 2, 4 (M 3) |
| Understands and uses negation with operators. | Ch 2 (M 3) |
| Uses and manipulates one-dimensional data structures. | Ch 4 (M 2, 3) |
| Detects and corrects syntactical errors. | Ch 2, 4 (M 1, 2, 3) |
| **Data & Data Representation** | |
| Understands how numbers, images, sounds and character sets use the same bit patterns. | Ch 3, (M 2, 3); Ch 5 (M 3) |
| Performs simple operations using bit patterns e.g. binary addition. | Ch 3 (M 2) |
| Understands the relationship between resolution and colour depth, including the effect on file size. | Ch 5 (M 3) |
| Distinguishes between data used in a simple program (a variable) and the storage structure for that data. | Ch 3 (M 2) |

| | |
|---|---|
| **Hardware & Processing** | |
| Understands the von Neumann architecture in relation to the fetch-execute cycle, including how data is stored in memory. | Ch 3 (M 3) |
| Understands the basic function and operation of location addressable memory. | Ch 3 (M 3) |
| **Communication & Networks** | |
| Knows the names of hardware e.g. hubs, routers, switches, and the names of protocols e.g. SMTP, IMAP, POP, FTP, TCP/IP, associated with networking computer systems. | Ch 5 (M 1, 2) |
| Uses technologies and online services securely, and knows how to identify and report inappropriate conduct. | Ch 5 (M 1, 2); Ch 6 (M 3) |
| **Information Technology** | |
| Evaluates the trustworthiness of digital content and considers the usability of visual design features when designing and creating digital artefacts for a known audience. | Ch 6 (M 3) |
| Identifies and explains how the use of technology can impact on society. | Ch 6 (M 3) |
| Designs criteria for users to evaluate the quality of solutions, uses the feedback from the users to identify improvements and can make appropriate refinements to the solution. | Ch 6 (M 3) |
| **Black objectives** | **Matrix books (M)** |
| **Algorithms** | |
| Recognises that the design of an algorithm is distinct from its expression in a programming language (which will depend on the programming constructs available). | Ch 1 (M 2, 3); Ch 4 (M 1, 2, 3) |
| Evaluates the effectiveness of algorithms and models for similar problems. | Ch 1 (M 1, 2, 3) |
| Recognises where information can be filtered out in generalising problem solutions. | Ch 1 (M 1, 2, 3) |
| Uses logical reasoning to explain how an algorithm works. | Ch 1 (M 1, 2, 3) |
| Represents algorithms using structured language. | Ch 1 (M 1, 2, 3) |
| **Programming & Development** | |
| Appreciates the effect of the scope of a variable e.g. a local variable can't be accessed from outside its function. | Ch 4 (M 3) |
| Understands and applies parameter passing. | Ch 4 (M 3) |
| Understands the difference between, and uses, both pre-tested e.g. 'while', and post-tested e.g. 'until' loops. | Ch 4 (M 2, 3) Ch 1 (M 2) |
| Applies a modular approach to error detection and correction. | Ch 4 (M 3) |
| **Data & Data Representation** | |
| Knows the relationship between data representation and data quality. | Ch 5 (M 3) |
| Understands the relationship between binary and electrical circuits, including Boolean logic. | Ch 3 (M 2, 3) |
| Understands how and why values are data typed in many different languages when manipulated within programs. | Ch 4 (M 3) |
| **Hardware & Processing** | |
| Knows that processors have instruction sets and that these relate to low-level instructions carried out by a computer. | Ch 3 (M 3) |
| **Communication & Networks** | |
| Knows the purpose of the hardware and protocols associated with networking computer systems. | Ch 5 (M 2, 3) |
| Understands the client-server model, including how dynamic web pages use server-side scripting, and that web servers process and store data entered by users. | Ch 5 (M 3) |
| Recognises that persistence of data on the Internet requires careful protection of online identity and privacy. | Ch 5 (M 2, 3) |
| **Information Technology** | |
| Undertakes creative projects that collect, analyse, and evaluate data to meet the needs of a known user group. | Ch 6 (M 1,2, 3) |
| Effectively designs and creates digital artefacts for a wider or remote audience. | Ch 2, 4, 6 (M 1, 2, 3) |
| Considers the properties of media when importing them into digital artefacts. | Ch 2 (M 1); Ch 6 (M 2); Ch 5 (M 3) |
| Documents user feedback, the improvements identified and the refinements made to the solution. | Ch 6 (M 3) |
| Explains and justifies how the use of technology impacts on society, from the perspective of social, economical, political, legal, ethical and moral issues. | Ch 6 (M 3) |

# What students will do in each chapter of *Matrix 3*

## Chapter 1: Computational Thinking

*Students use computer models to test, understand, predict and teach others about how real-world systems behave. In this chapter, students model the effects of radioactive leaks on the environment. They also model the effects of the half-life of radioactive medicines on patient care.*

| | |
|---|---|
| Computing POS | Design, use and evaluate computational abstractions that model the state and behaviour of real-world problems and physical systems; Understand several key algorithms that reflect computational thinking. |
| CAS | Understand the notion of performance for algorithms and appreciate that some algorithms have different performance characteristics for the same task.<br><br>Extended learning: Represent algorithms using structured language. |

## Chapter 2: App Inventor

*Students make a game that they can play on a mobile phone, a tablet or a desktop computer with a mouse.*

| | |
|---|---|
| Computing POS | Use at least two programming languages, one of which is textual, to solve a variety of computational problems; Create digital artefacts for a given audience; Design and develop modular programs that use procedures or functions. |
| CAS | Use a range of operators and expressions e.g. Boolean, and apply them in the context of program control; Use nested selection statements; Appreciate the effect of the scope of a variable e.g. a local variable can't be accessed from outside its function. |

## Chapter 3: Data and the CPU

*Students find out how a computer works. They revise the main parts of the computer, learn more about the CPU and how memory works.*

| | |
|---|---|
| Computing POS | Understand simple Boolean logic [for example, AND, OR and NOT] and some of its uses in circuits; Understand how instructions are stored and executed within a computer system. |
| CAS | Recognise and understand the function of the main internal parts of basic computer architecture; Understand the concepts behind the fetch-execute cycle; Understand the von Neumann architecture in relation to the fetch-execute cycle, including how data is stored in memory; Understand the basic function and operation of location addressable memory; Understand the relationship between binary and electrical circuits, including Boolean logic. |

## Chapter 4: Introducing Python

*Students write a program in Python to store names. The program can be used by anyone who manages a group of people such as a team coach, teacher or orchestra leader.*

| | |
|---|---|
| Computing POS | Use at least two programming languages, one of which is textual, to solve a variety of computational problems; Design and develop modular programs that use procedures or functions; Create digital artefacts for a given audience. |
| CAS | Have practical experience of a high-level textual language, including using standard libraries when programming; Use a range of operators and expressions e.g. Boolean, and apply them in the context of program control; Select the appropriate data types; Define data types: real numbers and Boolean; Appreciate the need for, and write, custom functions including use of parameters; Understand and apply parameter passing; Apply a modular approach to error detection and correction; Use nested selection statements. |

## Chapter 5: Information Technology

*Students learn how computers store text, image and audio data. They also find out how and why data files are compressed. They discover how to keep data safe by creating and using strong passwords.*

| | |
|---|---|
| Computing POS | Understand how data of various types (including text sounds and pictures) can be represented and manipulated digitally, in the form of binary digits. |
| CAS | Understand how numbers, images, sounds and character sets use the same bit patterns; Understand the relationship between resolution and colour depth, including the effect on file size; Know the relationship between data representation and data quality.<br><br>Extended learning: Understand the client-server model including how dynamic web pages use server-side scripting and that web servers process and store data entered by users. |

## Chapter 6: Creative Communication

*Students work together using technology, creating forms, slideshows and reports. They also learn about copyright and plagiarism, to help them understand how to use the Internet responsibly.*

| | |
|---|---|
| Computing POS | Undertake creative projects that involve selecting, using and combining multiple applications to achieve challenging goals; Create digital artefacts for a given audience; Meet the needs of known users with attention to trustworthiness, design and usability; Re-use, revise and re-purpose digital artefacts for a given audience including collecting and analysing data. |
| CAS | Recognise ethical issues surrounding the application of information technology beyond school; Identify and explain how the use of technology can impact on society; Design criteria for users to evaluate the quality of solutions, use the feedback from the users to identify improvements and can make appropriate refinements to the solution; Effectively design and create digital artefacts for a wider or remote audience; Document user feedback, the improvements identified and the refinements made to the solution.<br><br>Extended learning: Explain and justify how the use of technology impacts on society, from the perspective of social, economic, political, legal, ethical and moral issues. |

# Preparing the programming languages

Students will work with two different programming languages in *Matrix 3*:

- App Inventor
- Python.

## Preparing to use App Inventor

App Inventor is a lively, visual language that is used in classrooms all over the world. It is hosted by MIT (Massachusetts Institute of Technology). App Inventor is freely available for you and your students to use in class or at home. No prior experience is needed to use App Inventor.

These are key facts about App Inventor.

- **App Inventor is cloud-based:** You open App Inventor in your Internet browser. Your work is saved on a remote server—not on your own computer.
- **To log in to App Inventor you need to have a Google Account:** All users of Gmail, for example, can use their Gmail login. Google accounts are free to set up. Some students may already have Gmail logins. You may set up additional accounts for students in your class.
- **You can run completed programs on an Android device or an on-screen emulator:** You will need to have one or both of these set up so students can run their completed programs.

### Choose the right browser

You work on App Inventor by connecting to the website with a browser. The App Inventor team recommend that you use Firefox or Google Chrome to connect to App Inventor. Internet Explorer is not recommended.

To create a Google account, visit:

`https://accounts.google.com/signup`

You may create a group of accounts for your school, or encourage students to set up their own Google accounts individually. Make sure students remember their passwords.

- App Inventor website:
  `http://appinventor.mit.edu/`
- The App Inventor software is available at this URL. You will find any programs you and your students have made at this location.
  `http://ai2.appinventor.mit.edu/`
- Getting Started page:
  `http://appinventor.mit.edu/explore/get-started.html`

## Use an Android device

Once they have made their apps, students can run them on any Android device, such as a mobile phone or tablet. Students can use their own phones. This is a lively and exciting way for students to see their work come to life on their phone. You may want to have two or three spare Android phones or tablets in the classroom for students who do not have Android phones.

To run your app on an Android phone, make sure that:

↗ your computer is connected to a wireless network

↗ the phone is connected to the same wireless network

↗ the App Inventor Companion is installed on the phone.

To find out more and download the App Inventor Companion:

`http://appinventor.mit.edu/explore/ai2/setup-device-wifi.html`

You can run any app you make from the project screen. Open the Connect menu and select AI Companion.

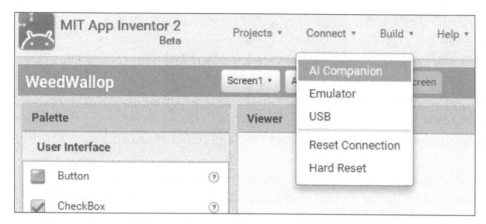

You will see a window like this.

The pattern is called a QR code. You can scan the QR code or enter the text code. The App should appear on the screen of your device.

## Use the emulator

If you cannot use an Android device, the second best option is to use an emulator. The emulator looks like the screen of a mobile phone on your computer screen. You will see your app running on the screen. Many schools develop mainly on emulators and provide a few Android devices for final testing. You will have to install some software on your school computers called aiStarter.

Find out more about the emulator:

`http://appinventor.mit.edu/explore/ai2/setup-emulator.html`

If you are not sure whether to use the AI Companion or the emulator, discuss the options with your school technician or network administrator.

## Further information

There is a variety of information on the App Inventor website.

- Support for teachers:
  `http://teach.appinventor.mit.edu/`
- Trouble-shooting connection issues:
  `http://appinventor.mit.edu/explore/ai2/connection-help.html`
- Full online documentation:
  `http://appinventor.mit.edu/explore/library.html`
- A document for school technicians:
  `https://docs.google.com/document/d/1GMXO_GoCRj3052Pg93dzEzJ5sXido`
  `9U17Xrn6HYU6Xs/edit`

Make sure you test the App Inventor connection before you use it with your students. Occasionally, organisational security settings, such as an Internet firewall, can interfere with the use of online services such as App Inventor. If you experience problems when you first use App Inventor discuss this with your chief technician or head of IT.

# Preparing to use Python

Python is a straightforward text-based programming language. Python can be downloaded for free and used on any computer without restriction. Go through the exercises and activities in the *Matrix* Student Book. In doing this, you will develop enough confidence and skills to lead students through the fundamentals of Python.

To download a copy of Python visit:

`https://www.python.org`

You will see links to the area of the site to download the files you need to write and run Python programs. At the time of writing the URL for this area was:

`https://www.python.org/downloads/`

You or your school or college technician can also use this link to download and install Python on all classroom computers.

## Versions

More than one version of Python is available on the website. Python version numbers are constantly updated. However, differences between recent versions are minor, and it will not matter which version you use. Simply download the most up-to-date version available on the site.

Note: There are significant differences between versions of Python which begin with '2' (e.g. Python 2.3.1.) and those which begin with '3' (e.g. Python 3.4.4.). This book is written for any version of Python which begins with 3.

# Differentiation and assessment of learning

The *Matrix* series focuses support for a range of students and includes supporting students who may struggle with challenging English-language content. This focus means that most students will achieve curriculum targets by working through the content of the books. It also means that confident and able students will be able to extend their understanding and demonstrate that understanding through extension activities and independent work.

You can assess students' progress by observing their completion of the learning activities (**Now you do it...** ) for each lesson. The short test questions (**Test yourself...** ) at the end of each lesson give you an additional opportunity to confirm progress and differentiate between students working at different levels. The test questions in each lesson are differentiated and colour-coded. The questions with the blue panel are for the Foundation level. The questions with the green panel are Extension questions.

In classes where most students have limited English, you may find that many fall into the 'needing support' category.

**DEVELOPING UNDERSTANDING (students needing support):** Some students may need several classroom sessions to complete a single lesson activity. These students may achieve only some of the goals set. This is better than rushing them to finish all set tasks without full understanding. Support students to complete as many learning activities as they can manage. Encourage students to at least complete the Foundation questions in the short test (**Test yourself...** ) section.

**SECURING UNDERSTANDING (most students):** Most students will be able to follow the activities in each lesson, completing this work in one lesson, and answering the test questions that follow. The completion of practical work and answers to these questions will provide practical and written evidence of learning. Students with good English skills may be able to work from the guidance in the books. These students should successfully complete all Foundation questions and attempt Extension questions.

**EXTENDING UNDERSTANDING (more-able students):** Students who work with confidence will be able to complete activities working from the instruction in the book. They will have time to complete the extension activities (**If you have time...** ) included with each lesson. Model answers to these activities are provided in the lesson guides that follow. Students should successfully complete the ten short test questions and the Starter to Extension activities in the review section at the end of the chapter. The extended test in the review section will give you the opportunity to check students' retention of skills and knowledge, and differentiate achievement. Practical activities at Starter, Intermediate and Extension level are included. Students should attempt as many of these as they can to show their understanding.

## Summary of differentiation

| | In a typical classroom session | Activities | Short tests | End-of-topic review |
|---|---|---|---|---|
| Students needing support or with language issues | May complete part of the content of one lesson. | May need help to complete the learning activity. | Will attempt the Foundation questions. | Will attempt the end-of-topic test. Will complete the Starter activity. |
| Most students | Will cover the learning and skills content of one lesson. | Will complete the learning activity, working independently. May complete the Extension activity. | Will attempt all questions, getting all or most correct. | Will answer all questions in the end-of-topic test. Will complete the Starter and Intermediate activities. If there is time, may attempt the Extension activity. |
| More-able students | Will cover all of one lesson including additional content linked to extension work. May move onto further lessons. | Will complete the main and Extension activities. | Will answer all questions correctly. | Will answer all questions correctly in the end-of-topic test. Will complete all activities. |

## Curriculum coverage

This chapter covers part or all of the requirements for the Computing Programme of Study (age 11–14) for England:

↗ design, use and evaluate computational abstractions that model the state and behaviour of real-world problems and physical systems

↗ understand several key algorithms that reflect computational thinking.

This chapter also covers these main requirements for the Computing at School (CAS) Progression Pathways (for a full list of requirements met, see pages 9–10 of this handbook):

↗ understand the notion of performance for algorithms and appreciate that some algorithms have different performance characteristics for the same task.

CAS extension:

↗ represent algorithms using structured language.

## Preparation

Read the Student Book for this chapter before you begin this topic. Make sure you understand what students should already know, and that you are confident in your understanding of the key terms and concepts introduced in this chapter.

## Learning outcomes

In this chapter students use computational thinking to model and understand the way in which nuclear power and nuclear medicine affect our lives. They are guided step by step through every part of the activities in the chapter. They are introduced to new terms and ways of representing problems. Most importantly, students apply their developing computational skills to modelling a set of real-world problems.

By completing this chapter students will be able to:

- decompose a problem
- identify variables
- use processes, inputs and outputs in computational thinking
- design a computational abstraction
- use a computational abstraction
- evaluate a computational abstraction
- understand the difference between an input variable and a set variable in computer modelling
- understand how abstractions model things in the real world.

## Going nuclear

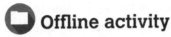 Offline activity

All of the activities in this chapter are based on simple ideas about nuclear power and nuclear medicine. In order for students to enjoy working on these models, they need a basic understanding of what the term 'nuclear' means.

The offline activity introduces some key ideas to help students develop this understanding. Students stand together closely in a group. Each student in the group has two paper balls. One student begins by throwing the first paper ball into the group. If the ball hits a student, that students throws both of his or her paper balls in the air. As more balls hit more students more balls are thrown into the air. This activity is a model for how nuclear fission works. Atoms are hit by neutrons, just as students are hit by paper balls. The atoms release their own neutrons, just as students throw their paper balls into the air. The neutrons are a form of energy. We can use that energy in many different ways in modern life.

**Talk about...**

The discussion is also an activity you can do offline. You could use this activity any time to vary the pace of lessons and encourage students to reflect on their learning.

Begin the discussion by reading the text on page 6 of the Student Book. Give students one example of each of the ways we can use computer models. Here are some examples. We can use a computer model to:

- test parts for a space rocket without having to build them and send them to space
- explain how the solar system works
- predict what might happen if we give a type of medicine to a person with a virus
- teach others about the way the liver works.

Working either as a whole class or in groups, ask students to think of other real-life examples where we use computer models to test, understand, predict and teach others. Encourage students to talk about their thinking and decision-making processes. It is also an opportunity for those with English as an additional language to practise talking about their ideas.

## FACT

The Fact box gives students a little more information about nuclear power. Encourage them to think about the scale of different types of nuclear uses. The amount of boiling or pressurised water needed to run a nuclear power plant is huge. In contrast, nuclear medicine sometimes uses microscopic doses of nuclear material in order to diagnose or target illness.

Some students may be interested in learning more about nuclear uses. If your school's Acceptable Use Policy allows this, they could search the web using a browser, or an online video channel. Students could search using terms such as 'nuclear power' or 'nuclear medicine'.

## Word cloud

The Word cloud contains all the key words that are highlighted and defined in Key words boxes in the lessons. The key words for this chapter are: assumptions, decomposition, modelling, variable, abstraction, input, iteration, output, process, representation, pseudocode and time steps.

### Learning outcomes

When they have completed this lesson students should be able to:

- ↗ decompose a problem
- ↗ identify a variable.

More-confident students will:

- ↗ evaluate their computational thinking.

## Overview

In this lesson students are introduced to the idea of a computer model. Students begin the chapter project by decomposing a problem based on the idea of a nuclear reactor leaking into the environment, and identifying the variables that are needed to solve the problem.

## Language development

This lesson reminds students that in computational thinking we use algorithms to solve problems. The first step in solving a problem is to decompose the problem into smaller parts.

The lesson introduces students to two new terms.

- **Model:** A model is a way of representing things, processes and systems. We can use a computer model to understand a complicated system and predict what might happen. We can also test ideas without needing to build real-life examples, and use what we know about one system to help us understand another.

- **Variable:** In order to develop a model based on good computational thinking, we need to identify the variables in the model. A variable is anything that can be changed, controlled and measured in a model. Students may have heard the term 'variable' in natural science lessons. The word has the same meaning in computational science.

## Before the lesson

Think about some examples of computer models that will suit students and their setting. Students may need many examples to understand what a computer model is. These examples will also help them understand how they can use their computational thinking to solve modelling problems.

For example, if you live in a country with distinctive weather patterns, you could talk about how computer models can be used to predict rainfall. Be prepared to ask students why this might be important to farmers or builders, for example.

The key words for this lesson are: assumptions, decomposition, modelling and variable. The words are highlighted in the text the first time they appear. Their definitions are included in the Key words box at the end of the lesson. You may want to review these words before the lesson.

## ⌘ Learn about...

You will lead the first part of the lesson. Make sure students understand these ideas. You may ask them to make notes. You may use directed questioning to check understanding.

- Computational thinking is a way of solving problems. There are many tools in our computational thinking toolset.

- In this chapter students will learn about another tool called a model, or modelling. We can use models to understand many real-life problems.

- Modelling is useful because computers are powerful and can handle a large amount of information, or data. A computer model uses algorithms to help use data to solve problems.

- In order to develop a computer model, we need to identify the variables that we can change, control or measure. For example, in a computer game a variable is the number of 'lives' you have before you must restart a level.

##  How to...

In the second part of the lesson students complete an exercise under your guidance. The exercise sets out the important questions students will answer during the first four lessons of this chapter. Highlight the following points to students.

- We start solving computational thinking problems by decomposing the problem.
- The Student Book gives an example of an environmental model in which students need to understand how a herd of elephants behaves in a habitat. Ask students to think about who might find this information useful (e.g. park rangers, conservationists or people living near a game reserve).
- Talk about the kinds of questions you can ask to decompose a modelling problem. For students who have English as an additional language, highlight the question starter words and phrases they can use. These might include: 'how many', 'what', 'where', 'are there/they', 'is there'. Ask students to think about questions that are important to the problem, and questions that are not important.
- We can use the decomposed questions to help identify the variables in the problems.

 ## Now you do it...

Explain that for the first four lessons of this chapter, students will model what happens when a nuclear reactor leaks into the environment. In this lesson students think about the problem of a nuclear reactor leaking into a water pond.

**What success looks like:** In groups, students decompose the problem, taking into account the assumptions on page 11. There will be a range of answers, but most should include the following.

- There is radioactivity leaking into the pond.
- There is radioactive decay, leading to a reduction in radioactivity in the pond.

These are other possible answers.

- The pond could have plants or fish living in it.
- There might be rainfall into the pond.
- Water might be flowing out of the pond or evaporation could be taking place.

The Student Book asks students to identify variables for the problem. The most important variable is the amount of radioactivity in the pond. Other variables could include:

- the size of the pond
- plant or fish life affected by the radiation.

 ## If you have time...

Individual student groups evaluate the thinking of another group to improve their own work.

**What success looks like:** A good evaluation shows that students have thought about whether the computational thinking is decomposed, efficient, elegant and correct. Their feedback is focused on the work, shows where things are working well, and is specific.

## Test yourself...

FOUNDATION QUESTIONS

1  Why is modelling important in modern life? Answer: We can use computer models to understand difficult systems, objects or processes.

2  Why are computers useful for modelling? Answer: Computers are powerful. They can handle a lot of data or information. We can use these data or information to solve problems.

EXTENSION QUESTIONS

Imagine you have been asked to create a computer model of the way a fire spreads through a forest.

3  Decompose the problem. Students will need to think about where the fire burns and the conditions surrounding the fire. Possible answers include: spread of fire from one part of the forest to nearby parts of the forest; the shape and structure of the forest (as this will affect where and how fast the fire can go); whether there are rivers, streams, clearings or sandbanks that would block the fire; weather conditions.

4  Identify the variables you would need to create the model. Possible answers include: how fast the fire can travel; where the fire can travel; the amount of fire at any given place in the forest.

## Learning outcomes

When they have completed this lesson students should be able to:

↗ use processes

↗ use inputs and outputs

More-confident students will:

↗ represent their thinking using pseudocode.

## Overview

In this lesson students learn about processes, inputs and outputs in computer modelling. They learn how to use a diagram to show how their model could work. This builds on the abstraction students learned how to do in *Matrix 2*, Chapter 1, Computational thinking.

## Language development

Students may know from *Matrix 2* that abstraction is a tool. Abstraction helps us to remove unnecessary information in a problem or task. In this lesson students learn how to represent their abstraction in a diagram.

Students also learn some new terms in this lesson. In order to carry out the task, students need to understand that:

- a process is something that happens to make variables change in a computational thinking problem
- an input is a type of process that enters the computer model to change the variables
- an output is a type of process that leaves the model to change the variables.

## Before the lesson

Review the group work from Lesson 1.1. You may want to move students into new groups for this lesson. There is a lot of group work in this chapter. This is because working as a group to create solutions is an important skill for anyone planning a career in computing.

The key words for this lesson are: abstraction, input, iteration, output, process and representation. The words are highlighted in the text the first time they appear. Their definitions are included in the Key words box at the end of the lesson. You may want to review these words before the lesson.

## ⌘ Learn about...

You will lead the first part of the lesson. Make sure students understand these ideas. You may ask them to make notes. You may use directed questioning to check understanding.

- A process is something that happens in a computer model to make the variables change. Give students some real-life examples of processes. These might include pouring hot water on ice or exploring what happens to a virus when a sick person is given medicine.
- Inputs and outputs are types of process in a model. We can change variables in a problem by changing the inputs and outputs. In the example of a sick person receiving medicine, the medicine is an input. What happens to the person's symptoms is an output.

## ⏻ How to...

In the second part of the lesson students complete an exercise under your guidance. Remind students of the problem.

- What is the rate at which material is leaking into the pond?
- What is the rate at which the radioactive material decays?

Remind students of the work they have done to identify the variables in the problem. Students are asked to focus on one variable and two processes.

- The amount of radioactivity in the pond—this is the variable.
- An increase in radioactivity because of the leak—this is an input process.
- A decrease in the radioactivity because of the decay—this is an output process.

Encourage students to think about how the variable and processes affect each other. If students need extra help, ask them to act out the problem in their groups.

Show students how the diagram on page 14 represents the problem. Discuss with students why a representation like this might be useful. Encourage them to think of the diagram as a way of representing their abstracted ideas.

## ⊕ Now you do it...

Students work in groups—either the same groups as in Lesson 1.1 or different groups. Students create a flow chart to show what is happening in the problem, or model.

**What success looks like:** There may be a range of answers. Most answers should have the following parts:

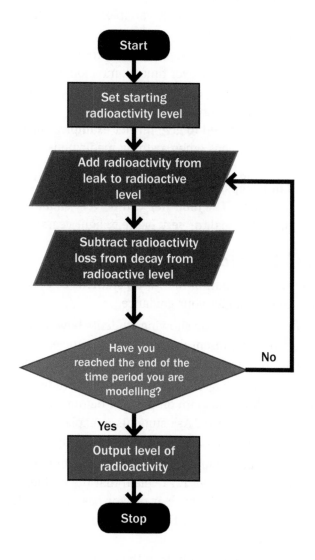

## 🌐 If you have time...

Students use pseudocode to show what happens in their model. Note: Due to column space in this handbook, long lines of pseudocode may run on to the next line. You can recognise this because the new line does not start with a capital letter.

**What success looks like:** Example answer:

```
SET (variable) amount_of_radioactivity =
starting amount of radioactivity
REPEAT
    Add radioactivity from leak to
    (variable) amount_of_radioactivity
    Subtract radioactivity loss from
    (variable) amount_of_radioactivity
UNTIL end of period you are modelling
OUTPUT (variable) amount_of_
radioactivity
```

##  Test yourself...

FOUNDATION QUESTIONS

**1** What is the difference between an input and an output? Answer: An input comes into a model. An output goes out of a model.

**2** How do processes and variables relate to each other? Answer: Processes change variables.

EXTENSION QUESTIONS

Imagine you are a computer game designer. You are designing a game in which letters appear on the screen. The player makes words from these letters. The letters then disappear and new letters appear on the screen.

**3** What are the processes and variables you need to think through for this game? There are several correct answers, including:
  - ○ **Processes:** choice of letters to appear; appearance of the letters; removal of words or letters; checking the word is a real word; working out score points for a word; increasing players' scores; time limit for completing a word
  - ○ **Variables:** time elapsed; score; dictionary of allowed words; word being considered; list of letters on the screen.

**4** What are the inputs and outputs you need to think through for this game? There are several correct answers, including:
  - ○ **Inputs:** letter combination; word produced by player
  - ○ **Outputs:** putting letters on the screen; whether the word is allowed or correct; current score.

## Learning outcomes

When they have completed this lesson students should be able to:

↗ decompose the complex problem of a nuclear reactor dump

↗ identify suitable variables to use in a model that includes changes

↗ use processes, inputs and outputs for a model that includes changes.

More-confident students will:

↗ use the Internet to find out more information about the nuclear reactor problem.

## Overview

In this lesson students look at a different nuclear reactor problem and the way it affects an environment. In the previous model, students worked on the problem of a steady leak into a pond over a period of time. In this model, students work on the problem of a sudden explosion of nuclear material onto a field.

## Language development

There are two key words used in this lesson. The first is 'pseudocode'. Students who have completed the other *Matrix* books will understand pseudocode and how we use it to communicate computational thinking. Pseudocode is a way to describe algorithms using words instead of a diagram (e.g. a flow chart).

The second key word is 'time steps'. A time step is a small change that happens in an equation, an algorithm or a model. We use time steps to model changes in a system over time.

## Before the lesson

If there are students who have not previously learned about pseudocode, you may want to bring this group together to introduce them to the key concepts. You could also pair them with confident pseudocode users during the lesson. Encourage more-confident students to explain their understanding.

## ⌘ Learn about...

You will lead the first part of the lesson. Make sure students understand these ideas. You may ask them to make notes. You may use directed questioning to check understanding.

- **Variable:** A variable is anything that can be changed, controlled and measured in a computer model.

- **Process:** A process is something that happens in a computer model to make the variables change. Inputs and outputs are types of processes in a model. We can change variables in a problem by changing the inputs and outputs.

- **Models:** Some models explore problems that change steadily over time. Some models explore problems where something happens suddenly. Students are given examples of sudden changes. They are asked to give further examples, such as what happens when a strong medicine is injected into a human body.

- **Time steps:** We use time steps to model changes over time. The time step can be very small (e.g. nanoseconds), or very big (e.g. light years).

## ⏻ How to...

In the second part of the lesson students complete an exercise under your guidance.

Start the exercise by showing students how to use a diagram to represent the problem of a nuclear reactor dumping nuclear waste onto a nearby field.

Compare the diagram on page 17 of the Student Book with the diagram on page 14 before reading the text on page 18. Ask students to explain what they see. Students may notice the following.

- There are no inputs into the problem in the diagram on page 17. Explain that the problem begins after the nuclear reactor has dumped the waste. This is why there is no input in this diagram.

- There are two outputs in the diagram on page 17, compared to one output in the diagram on page 14. Explain that this is because the nuclear waste has been dumped into a field. Nuclear waste will lose radioactivity through radioactive decay, and also through radioactive material in the harvest.

Check whether students were correct using the information on page 18.

The learning activity shows students how to use pseudocode to illustrate how the model would work. Point out:

- the time step of one year, because the field is likely to be harvested annually

- the two outputs (decay and harvest).

##  Now you do it...

Students decompose the problem, write a list of variables and create a flow chart.

**What success looks like:**

1 Decompose the radioactive field problem. Answer: initial amount of radioactivity; loss of radioactivity through decay; loss of radioactivity through harvest; the safe level of radioactivity in a crop.

2 Write a list of variables. Answer: The most important variable is the amount of radioactivity

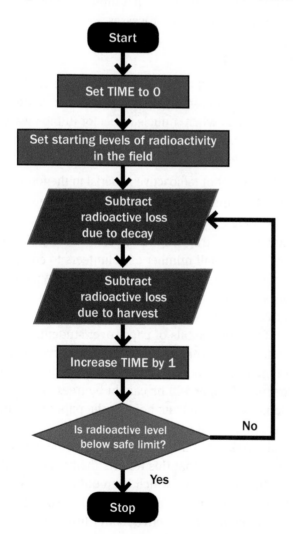

in the field. Students may also include: size of the field, rainfall, strong winds and types of plant growing in the field.

3 Create a flow chart to represent the model. An example flow chart is shown below in the left-hand column.

## If you have time...

Students use the Internet to find out what level of radioactivity is safe in crops grown for humans to eat.

**What success looks like:** There are several possible answers. The most important fact students should discover from their Internet search is that we absorb very small amounts of radiation every day. We measure radiation in units of Sieverts. Eating a banana can mean absorbing 0.1 Sievert units.

## Test yourself...

FOUNDATION QUESTIONS

**1** Decompose the problem of a dead whale's body falling to the ocean floor. Many creatures are able to feed from the body. We call these the feeding species. Several answers are possible, including: whale body falls; feeding species eat whale meat; the amount of whale meat decreases. Students might also include: feeder species reproduce; predator species are attracted and eat feeder species. This would be an unusually strong answer, and additional credit should be given.

**2** Can you identify the variables when you decompose the problem of a dead whale's body falling to the ocean floor? Answer: amount of whale meat left; number of feeding animals (e.g. fish).

EXTENSION QUESTIONS

**3** Can you identify the processes when you decompose the problem of a dead whale's body falling to the ocean floor? Answer: loss of the whale's body due to feeding; change in number of feeding animals. Students might notice that if the feeding species have plenty to eat, they will reproduce, so there will be more feeders, and so the rate at which the whale's body is broken down increases.

**4** Would you use a time step to model this problem? If you would use a time step, how long do you think it should be? Answer: Yes, a time step is useful. It should be long enough to describe loss of whale meat over time, but short enough to describe possible changes in the number of feeder species because of reproduction or being eaten by predators.

### Learning outcomes

When they have completed this lesson students should be able to:

↗ design a computational abstraction

↗ use a computational abstraction

↗ evaluate a computational abstraction

↗ understand how abstractions model things in the real world.

More-confident students will:

↗ use the Internet to find out more information about the problem they are modelling.

## Overview

In this lesson students carry out the most difficult modelling exercise of this chapter. This is the last nuclear reactor model students will develop. Students think about what happens after a nuclear reactor dumps radioactive waste into a forest.

This lesson is designed to extend more-confident students. You could use the lesson to spend additional time with students who are struggling in order to help them catch up, while more-confident students support one another.

## Before the lesson

Review students' responses to the 'Test yourself... ' questions in previous lessons. Make a list of the students who are finding the material challenging. Work with these students during this lesson to reinforce their understanding, and address any misunderstandings.

Encourage the most-confident students to try to write a short program to model the simpler problems in this chapter, outside the lesson.

If you would like to play the game in the 'How to... ' part of the lesson you will need lots of very small pieces of paper (e.g. confetti).

## ⌘ Learn about...

You will lead the first part of the lesson. Make sure students understand these ideas. You may ask them to make notes. You may use directed questioning to check understanding.

● Review the computational thinking stages in making a simple model of a problem. Remind students of the problems they have already modelled. These problems have one variable,

such as the amount of radioactive material in a pond or a field.

● Remind students how to identify inputs. For example, students have identified a radioactive leak into a pond. They have also learned how to identify outputs. For example, they have identified radioactive decay out of a field over time. Remind students that inputs and outputs are special kinds of processes.

## ⏻ How to...

In the second part of the lesson students complete an exercise under your guidance. Students model what happens when a nuclear reactor dumps waste onto a nearby forest. They model a problem with two variables:

● the amount of radioactive material in the forest soil

● the amount of radioactive material in the trees in the forest.

If students are struggling to understand this, play a game. Ask a small number of volunteers to come to the front of the class. Some students lie down on the floor pretending to be soil, and some students stand like trees nearby. All students hold their hands open. Sprinkle the bits of paper over students for them to catch. Explain this is the radioactive matter from the nuclear power station. Show students that some bits of paper will be caught by trees, and some by soil. Ask the students holding the paper to let go of a small amount of paper each time you count a number. Ask the soil students to pass some paper to the trees. Explain that this reflects the behaviour of the radioactive decay, which is an output from both the soil and the trees. Explain that this also reflects the movement of radioactive matter from the soil into the trees through the roots.

Look at the diagram representing this model. Ask students to compare the diagrams on pages 20 and 21. Point out the inputs and outputs. Show students that each box represents one variable.

 ## Now you do it...

Students decompose the problem, write their assumptions, identify the variables and processes and represent the model in pseudocode.

**What success looks like:**

1 Decompose the radioactive forest problem. Answer: Amount of radioactivity in the soil; radioactivity going from the soil into the trees; radioactivity in the trees; radioactive decay in the soil; radioactive decay in the trees.

2 Write your assumptions. Answer: All of the radioactive material is dumped at once; all of the trees are taking up radioactive material at the same rate and amount; all areas of the forest are the same; rain has no effect. For additional credit: We are not considering the return of radioactive material from falling leaves into the ground.

3 Write a list of the variables and processes. Answer: There are two variables. 1) The amount of radioactivity in the soil. 2) The amount of radioactivity in the trees. There are three processes. 1) The radioactive decay in the soil. 2) The trees take up radioactive material from the soil. 3) Radioactive decay from the trees.

4 Represent the model using pseudocode. Answer:

```
SET (variable) amount_of_radioactivity
_in_soil = starting amount of
radioactivity

SET (variable) amount_of_radioactivity
_in_trees = zero

SET (variable) time = 0

REPEAT

    Subtract radioactivity loss from
    (variable) amount_of_radioactivity_
    in_soil

    Subtract radioactivity taken up
    from soil to trees from (variable)
    amount_of_radioactivity_in_soil

    Add radioactivity taken up from
    soil to trees to (variable) amount_
    of_radioactivity_in_trees
```

```
    Subtract radioactivity loss from
    (variable) amount_of_radioactivity_
    in_trees

    Increase (variable) time by 1

UNTIL end of period you are modelling

OUTPUT (variable) amount_of_
radioactivity_in_soil

OUTPUT (variable) amount_of_
radioactivity_in_trees
```

 ## If you have time...

Students answer the question 'How long do you think it would take for the forest to become safe? Use the Internet to help you.'

**What success looks like:** Several answers are possible, depending on the seriousness of the nuclear disaster. Students should read about the Chernobyl and Fukushima disasters on the Internet. The Chernobyl disaster shows us that forests are still not fully recovered decades after a nuclear accident occurs.

 ## Test yourself...

FOUNDATION QUESTIONS

1 Write the computational thinking steps you would use to create a simple model. Answer: 1. Decompose the problem. 2. Identify the assumptions. 3. Identify the variables. 4. Identify the processes. 5. Represent the problem in a diagram. 6. Explain your thinking.

2 Explain in your own words why each step is important. Answer. Several answers are possible. Most students should make these points.

- Decomposition is important because it breaks the problem down into smaller parts that are easier to solve.
- Assumptions help us to identify the most important variables.
- We need to know which variables can be changed, or are likely to change, in a problem.
- Processes change variables, so we need to be able to identify these to make sure our model is correct.
- Diagrams can be useful in showing an abstracted problem.
- We can use flow charts and pseudocode to explain our computational thinking to others.

## EXTENSION QUESTIONS

**3** In Lesson 1.3 you decomposed the problem of a dead whale's body falling to the ocean floor. Now draw a diagram to show what happens when the whale's body decomposes, in the same way as we drew a diagram to represent our pond and field models. Think about the creatures that are feeding off the body. Answer:

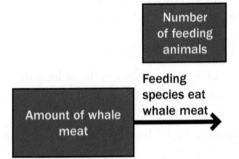

**4** Using pseudocode, write a simple model of what happens to the dead whale's body.

```
SET (variable) amount_of_whale_meat =
starting amount of whale meat
REPEAT
    Subtract amount of whale meat
    eaten from (variable) amount_of_
    whale_meat
UNTIL all whale meat is eaten
```

---

## 1.5 Nuclear medicine
pages 24–27

### Learning outcomes

When they have completed this lesson students should be able to:

↗ decompose a problem in the world of nuclear medicine

↗ identify variables and processes to use in this problem.

More-confident students will:

↗ use the Internet safely to find out more about nuclear medicine.

## Overview

In this lesson students apply their understanding of computational thinking in modelling problems to a new topic. Students find out about how we use radioactivity in medicine. Students need to have the opportunity to apply their understanding, knowledge and skills to different contexts. This will:

- reinforce their learning
- deepen their understanding
- help them explain their thinking to others.

## Language development

There are no new computational thinking terms introduced in this lesson. However, students are introduced to the scientific term 'half-life'. The half-life of a radioactive material is how long it takes for half of the atoms in the material to decay. This idea is important for Lessons 1.5 and 1.6.

## Before the lesson

If you think students may struggle to understand the term 'half-life', there are a number of good video tutorials and simulations on the Internet that explain the concept. Using a video channel accessible in your location, search for 'explain half-life' to find a suitable video for your class.

## ⌘ Learn about…

You will lead the first part of the lesson. Make sure students understand these ideas. You may ask them to make notes. You may use directed questioning to check understanding.

- We can use radioactive material in medicine. Radioactive material can be used to help diagnose illnesses, and to treat them.
- Different types of radioactive material treat different types of illness. Each type of radioactive material has a different half-life.
- Hospitals need to replace radioactive materials as these materials decay and lose their strength. Hospitals can work out how long radioactive materials will last by using a computer model. We can use our computational thinking to work out how to model this problem.

##  How to...

In the second part of the lesson students complete an exercise under your guidance. Students begin to think through the problem of how long Iodine-131 will last on a shelf until it needs to be replaced. Students:

- decompose the problem
- identify the two variables in the problem (the amount of radioactivity in the iodine and time)
- identify the process in the problem (radioactive decay).

## 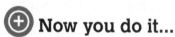 Now you do it...

Students carry out the same tasks for radioactive strontium.

**What success looks like:** Students should quickly see that that the decomposition, variables and process are identical for strontium and any other type of radioactive material. Students should identify the two variables in the problem (the amount of radioactivity in the strontium and time), and one process (radioactive decay).

Explain that one of the powerful characteristics of computational thinking is that we can use one solution to solve many different types of problem.

## If you have time...

Students use the Internet to find out ten facts about nuclear medicine.

**What success looks like**: There are many possible answers. For example, nuclear medicine can be used to:

- discover the severity of a disease or illness
- spot and diagnose diseases in their very early stages, meaning that people can be treated as quickly as possible
- work out how a heart attack has damaged the heart
- help make choices between different treatment options
- work out how well an organ (e.g. the heart or brain) is working, before or after a treatment
- help to identify exactly where very precise surgery (e.g. brain surgery) should take place
- identify infection.

##  Test yourself...

FOUNDATION QUESTIONS

**1** What is the important first step in any computational thinking problem? Answer: Decompose the problem.

**2** What is the difference between a process and a variable? Answer: A variable is anything that can be changed, controlled and measured in a computer model. A process is the thing that happens to make the variables change.

EXTENSION QUESTIONS

**3** What do you notice about all of the decompositions you have done in this lesson? Answer: The decompositions were all the same, even if based on a different radioactive material.

**4** What does this tell us about computational thinking as a way of solving real-world problems? Answer: We can use one solution or type of solution to solve more than one problem. This means computational thinking is an efficient and effective way to solve real-world problems.

### Learning outcomes

When they have completed this lesson students should be able to:

↗ design a computational abstraction in the context of nuclear medicine

↗ understand the difference between an input variable and a set variable in computer modelling.

More-confident students will:

↗ think about how they could use their existing pseudocode to solve a variation on the problem.

## Overview

In this lesson students continue to solve the problem faced by a hospital when working out when it needs to replace radioactive materials used in medicine. Students use the decomposition they completed in Lesson 1.5 to write pseudocode showing their algorithms.

## Before the lesson

This is the final lesson in the chapter. You may want to work with less-confident students during this lesson to ensure that they understand and complete all of the work in the chapter before the assessment.

## ⌘ Learn about...

You will lead the first part of the lesson. Make sure students understand these ideas. You may ask them to make notes. You may use directed questioning to check understanding.

- Different types of radioactive material decay at different rates and have different half-lives. When they decay, they lose their strength. To help people who are ill, the medicines need to be at the right strength.

- Hospitals need to work out how long medicines will be at the right strength before they have to be replaced.

- We can calculate when radioactive medicines will need to be replaced using a computer model based on the half-lives of the medicines. We can use computational thinking tools to work out the right computer model.

##  How to...

In the second part of the lesson students complete an exercise under your guidance. Students build on the decomposition and identification of variables and processes completed in Lesson 1.5. They use pseudocode to show an algorithm that addresses the problem a hospital might face in working out when to replace decaying Iodine-131. Highlight the following key points.

- The first input variable is the amount of radioactivity in the material that the hospital has bought. The first input variable has been called `amount_of_radioactivity` in the pseudocode.

- The second input variable is the minimum level of radioactivity that the Iodine-131 needs to have to be useful. The second input variable has been called `useful_level`.

- `SET (variable)` asks the computer to build a number into the program.

- The first set variable identifies the type of radioactive material we are using. Ask students to explain why this is important. Answer: This is important because different radioactive materials have different half-lives.

- The second set variable is set to zero as this model starts from the time the medicine comes into the hospital.

- Ask students to identify the time step and to discuss why we would increase the time by the half-life of the Iodine-131.

Now you do it...

Students work with a partner to write pseudocode to work out how long any type of radioactive material will last in a hospital. More-confident students could work on their own, or competitively.

**What success looks like:**

```
INPUT (variable) amount_of_radioactivity
= amount of radioactivity in material
bought by hospital
INPUT (variable) useful_level =
minimum level of radioactivity for the
material to be useful
SET (variable) half_life = half_life
of isotope used
SET (variable) time (in correct time
units) = 0
REPEAT
    Decrease amount_of_radioactivity by
    half
    Increase time by half_life
UNTIL amount_of_radioactivity is below
useful_level
OUTPUT time (in correct time units)
(i.e. the time taken to fall below the
useful level)
```

 If you have time...

Students consider how they might change the pseudocode to make it easier to work with different units of time.

**What success looks like:** More-confident students may notice that they used a phrase similar to 'correct time units' to make the pseudocode useful for any type of radioactivity.

 Test yourself...

FOUNDATION QUESTIONS

1 What is an input variable? Give an example of an input variable. Answer: An input variable has information that the program gets from users. An example of an input variable is users entering their age.

2 What is a set variable? Give an example of a set variable. Answer: A set variable has information built into the program. An example of a set variable is the half-life of radioactive iodine.

EXTENSION QUESTIONS

3 Describe the main difference between the two sets of pseudocode you used in this lesson. Answer: The pseudocode provided in the lesson works only for one type of radioactive material. The pseudocode written by students works for any type of radioactive material.

4 Which of the two sets of pseudocode would be most useful for a hospital? Explain your thinking. Answer: The pseudocode written by students is more useful because it can be used for any type of radioactive material.

The test questions and assessment activities give you an opportunity to evaluate students' understanding. The questions are shown here with possible answers.

## Model answers to test questions

1   What is decomposition, and why is it important in computational thinking? Answer: Decomposition is breaking a problem down into smaller parts. Decomposition is important in computational thinking because it makes problems more manageable and easier to solve.

2   What is abstraction, and why is it important in computational thinking? Answer: Abstraction is removing unnecessary or unimportant information in a problem. Abstraction is important in computational thinking because it helps identify patterns and the relevant parts of the problem.

3   What is representation, and why is it important in computational thinking? Answer: A representation is a diagram of a problem or a model. Representation is important in computational thinking because we can show in a single diagram what would take many words to explain.

4   What is a pattern, and why is it important in computational thinking? Answer: A pattern is the similarities and differences between items in a group or set. Pattern recognition is important in computational thinking because it helps us to find the right algorithms to solve common issues in a problem, or to see the relationships between parts of a problem.

5   What is a model? Answer: A model is a way of representing something: a process or a system. Modelling is important in computational thinking because we can use it to understand and solve complicated problems.

6   How can computational thinking help to model real-life problems? Answer: A computer model can show us how a theory or idea could work in real life. It can handle large amounts of information and, because computers are powerful, we can design complicated models of difficult problems.

7   Name two of the real-life problems you have modelled in this chapter. Answer: (Any two of the following): nuclear waste leak into a pond; nuclear waste dump into a field; nuclear waste dump into a forest; ensuring radioactive materials are the right strength to help people who are ill.

8   Give one example of another real-life problem you could model using computational thinking. Answer: Several answers are possible, such as modelling environmental or weather change, or movement of people, animals or money across systems. Credit should be given for any example that demonstrates students' understanding that modelling is useful for solving complicated problems.

9   What is the difference between a variable and a process in computational thinking? Answer: A variable is anything that can be changed, controlled and measured in a model. A process is something that happens to make the variables change.

10   What is the difference between an input variable and a set variable? Answer: An input variable has information that the program gets from the user. A set variable has information built into the program.

##  Model answers to assessment activities

Students are asked to work out how many years it would take for half the light bulbs in the school to stop working.

### Starter activity

All students should be able to complete this activity.

1   Decompose the problem.

2   What are the variables and processes in the problem?

**What success looks like:** Students decompose the problem: number of working light bulbs; number of years passing; loss of working light bulbs. They identify the variables in the problem as: number of working light bulbs and time in years. They identify the processes as: light bulbs stop working.

## Intermediate activity

Write pseudocode to ask a computer to model the problem.

**What success looks like:** Students' pseudocode should look something like this.

```
SET (variable) number_of_working_
light_bulbs = 300

SET (variable) time (in years) = 0

REPEAT

    SET (variable) light_bulbs_lost_
    this_year = 10% of (variable)
    number_of_working_light_bulbs

    Subtract (variable) light_bulbs_
    lost_this_year from (variable)
    number_of_working_light_bulbs

    Increase (variable) time by 1 year

UNTIL (variable) number_of_working_
light_bulbs equals 150

OUTPUT (variable) time (in years)
```

## Extension activity

After half the light bulbs have stopped working, the school finds money to buy 50 new light bulbs per year. Students change their pseudocode to ask a computer to work out how many years it would take for there to be 300 working light bulbs again.

**What success looks like:** Students' pseudocode should look something like this.

```
SET (variable) number_of_working_
light_bulbs = 150

SET (variable) time in years = 0

REPEAT

    SET (variable) light_bulbs_lost_
    this_year = 10% of (variable)
    number_of_working_light_bulbs

    Subtract (variable) light_bulbs_
    lost_this_year from (variable)
    number_of_working_light_bulbs

    Add 50 to (variable) number_of_
    working_light_bulbs

    Increase (variable) time by 1 year

UNTIL (variable) number_of_working_
light_bulbs is at least 300

OUTPUT (variable) time (in years)
```

# App Inventor

## Curriculum coverage

This chapter covers part or all of the requirements for the Computing Programme of Study (age 11–14) for England:

↗ use at least two programming languages to solve a variety of computational problems

↗ create digital artefacts for a given audience

↗ design and develop modular programs that use procedures or functions.

This chapter also covers these main requirements for the Computing at School (CAS) Progression Pathways (for a full list of requirements met, see pages 9–10 of this handbook):

↗ use a range of operators and expressions (e.g. Boolean) and apply them in the context of program control

↗ use nested selection statements

↗ appreciate the effect of the scope of a variable (e.g. a local variable can't be accessed from outside its function).

## Preparation

Read the section 'Preparing to use App Inventor' in the introduction to this handbook (page 12), before you begin this topic. Make sure you understand how students can log in to App Inventor. Also make sure you have IDs and logins to assign, or you are ready to lead students in creating their own logins. Students who are continuing their studies from *Matrix 1* and *Matrix 2* may already have login IDs.

You may have students who are new to App Inventor. It may be best for these students to read Chapter 2, App Inventor, in *Matrix 1* and *Matrix 2*. They should complete the tasks set out in these chapters before starting work on this chapter. More-able students may work quite quickly through these activities.

This chapter assumes basic understanding of programming in general and App Inventor in particular, taken from the previous books.

## Learning outcomes

By completing this chapter students will be able to:

- make a game with a sprite moving on a canvas
- use a timer to control events
- use x and y co-ordinates to position objects
- use a conditional (if) structure in their code
- make random numbers
- create and use procedures

- use and explain the difference between global and local variables
- store values and get values back from storage.

## Make a mobile game

###  Talk about...

The discussion does not require the computer. Discuss the topic before students start the activities or at any time during the chapter to vary the pace. Use this opportunity to encourage students to reflect on their learning.

This discussion topic combines well with the offline activity of designing a game. Students may talk about the games they like and what features the games have. In particular, focus on these points.

- **Types of input:** What do you do to interact with the game?
- **Types of output:** What does the game 'do'? (Images, sounds and vibrations are the most common outputs. What are specific outputs for this game?)

### Offline activity

The offline activity gives students a chance to do creative work without using computers. You could use this activity to introduce the App Inventor activities.

In this chapter students make a computer game. In this offline activity students can work in groups or individually to design a computer game. This task gives students a chance to reflect on interface design and on the actions the user will take. They may also reflect on how the game may respond to users' actions. Students' creative ideas need not be limited by their technical skills. This activity follows on well from the discussion topic.

Make this an open-ended activity. Students can add any fun or challenging features they like. For example, they might want to consider how virtual reality could improve their game. This is a creative exercise for students to think about what might be possible. Young people have strong imaginations and this will engage them with the development work in this chapter.

## FACT

People pay around 10 billion euros per year for games run on mobile devices. Many games are also free to download. The programmers make money from advertising and other items. Other items include in-app purchases (purchases made from within an app) and upgrades.

The source for this fact is `http://www.statista.com/statistics/292056/video-game-market-value-worldwide/`

The value of the game market is always increasing. You may like to:

● search for a more up-to-date figure
● convert this figure to a currency that is more meaningful to the students you teach.

However, the general principle is valid whatever figure you use. A huge amount of money is spent on games. People who make popular games can make a lot of money.

## A note on choosing a topic for the game

The examples given in this chapter relate to a game called Weed Wallop where players try to squish weeds that spring up at random on a lawn. However, with minor adaptations this game could look quite different. Some examples are given in the Student Book. Depending on the students you teach, you may want to suggest changes in the game. The moving target can be an animal, a plain shape, a symbol or whatever feature you or the students think is most suitable.

The principle is exactly the same. Only the sprite and the background colour or image on the interface will change. If in doubt, use Weed Wallop.

## Word cloud

The Word cloud contains all the key words that are highlighted and defined in Key words boxes in the lessons. The key words for this chapter are: canvas, maximum, minimum, sprite, call, procedures, random, trigger, timer event, conditional structure, default, fires, global variable, local variable, storage and tag.

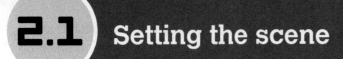

# 2.1 Setting the scene

## Learning outcomes

When they have completed this lesson students should be able to:

↗ make a game with a sprite moving on a canvas

↗ use x and y co-ordinates to position objects.

More-confident students will:

↗ extend and improve the interface design, think about users' needs and work independently.

## Overview

In this chapter students create a computer game. They use all the App Inventor skills they developed in previous books. They also learn new skills and demonstrate them. Each lesson builds on previous lessons. In this lesson students create an interface for the user to play the game. This also introduces the important new concept of defining a point using x and y co-ordinates.

## Language development

This lesson introduces the term 'sprite'. This term has a specific technical meaning: it is an object that moves on the screen, controlled by the computer program. Sprites are central to the development of computer games.

## Before the lesson

Make sure that all students are ready to use App Inventor, with working user logins. All students should have completed the simpler App Inventor tasks in *Matrix 1* and *Matrix 2*.

In this lesson students must find and upload an image to use as the sprite in their computer game. You may want to find one or more suitable image files that students can use. For example, you might look for images of dandelions and other weeds. Files in the JPEG (jay-peg) format are the most suitable.

The key words for this lesson are: canvas, maximum, minimum and sprite. The words are highlighted in the text the first time they appear. Their definitions are included in the Key words box at the end of the lesson. You may want to review these words before the lesson.

## 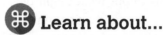 Learn about...

You will lead the first part of the lesson. Make sure students understand these ideas. You may ask them to make notes. You may use directed questioning to check understanding.

● **Plan the game:** Explain the general plan for the game. A sprite will appear on the screen. The player must try to squish the sprite by touching it on the screen to score points. In the Student Book example the user must squish weeds on a lawn. However, students might like to develop more dynamic ideas, such as featuring enemies or monsters.

● **Sprite and canvas:** The canvas is the background to the game. The sprite is the object that moves as you play the game. In this case, the sprite is an image of a dandelion, but you can pick any object you like.

● **x and y co-ordinates:** Explain how a point on a flat surface is designated using two numbers: the x and y co-ordinates. The x co-ordinate indicates how far to the left or right the point is. The y co-ordinate indicates how far up or down the point is.

● **Discussion:** Supervise a class or group discussion where students review their ideas for the game interface design. Images from cartoons or popular films make good targets. Avoid the use of images that might encourage cyber-bullying, such as pictures of students. This might be a useful opportunity to discuss what makes an appropriate image. Use your judgement about this.

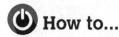 **How to...**

In the second part of the lesson students complete an exercise under your guidance. You may want to create an interface on screen, with students looking at what you do. The Student Book gives instructions.

- **Select media content:** Students should know how to find and upload suitable media files. They do this to upload a sprite image. Be aware that only some image formats will work with the App Inventor interface. JPEG is the most common of these formats. If in doubt, use JPEG format.

- **Create canvas:** The canvas is an object in the drawing and animation part of the App Inventor palette. Drag the canvas onto the Designer screen and set the size to fill the top part of the screen.

- **Add sprite:** Drag the sprite object onto the canvas. Using previous skills, students can link the sprite to the uploaded image. Set the size to be quite small (e.g. 50 pixels).

- **Investigate x and y co-ordinates:** Students can change the properties of objects in the Properties column. If they type a number for either the x or y co-ordinate, and press Enter, the sprite will move to that co-ordinate. This is a good way for students to learn the relationship between co-ordinates and position.

 **Now you do it...**

If students have followed your instructions, they should have created an interface with a canvas and a sprite. If necessary, take more than one lesson to complete this task. Ask more-confident students to start the extension activity as you support others who need help.

**What success looks like:** The Student Book shows several examples of interfaces. Students explain the minimum and maximum values for x and y co-ordinates on the canvas. In the example provided these values were 0 to 250 for both co-ordinates. Students should keep a note of these upper and lower values. They will use them in Lesson 2.2.

 **If you have time...**

Students who complete the task early and have explored the design of the interface may start a further task. They set the background image for the whole canvas. The background can be a photo or drawing instead of a plain background colour.

**What success looks like:** The Student Book shows an example of an interface with a background image. Any image that fills the canvas is proof that students have completed this task.

**Test yourself...**

FOUNDATION QUESTIONS

1. What is a sprite? Answer: A sprite is an image that can move about on a background. The movement of the sprite is controlled by the computer. Many computer games have sprites.

2. What values are represented by x and y co-ordinates? Answer: The x co-ordinate represents how far left or right a point is. The y co-ordinate represents how far up or down a point is.

EXTENSION QUESTIONS

3. Why do we give names to the components that we add to the interface? Answer: Giving names to components helps us when we need to refer to the components in our program code. Give extra credit if students mention that the name of an object can remind us what type of object it is (e.g. sprite or canvas).

4. Describe your game plan: what is your game called, and what image will you use as a sprite? Answer: This question gives students the chance to describe their plan for the game. The right answer will depend on each student's own plans. Give credit for a short but clear description of the game, a suitable name and a good choice of image.

### Learning outcomes

When they have completed this lesson students should be able to:

- ↗ use a timer to control events
- ↗ create and use a procedure
- ↗ make a random number.

More-confident students will:

- ↗ add a second sprite to the interface, working independently using the skills learned in this lesson.

## Overview

In Lesson 2.1 students created the interface for a game. The interface has one sprite. Students learned that the x and y co-ordinates set the position of the sprite. In this lesson students use random numbers to make the sprite move to a random place on the canvas.

## Language development

'Procedure' is a key technical term in programming. A procedure is a way of storing a set of commands. When you make a procedure you store a set of commands. You give the procedure a name. In the Student Book we say you 'make' the procedure. Programmers say they 'declare' the procedure.

When you use the procedure in your program, all the stored commands are carried out. Programmers say they 'call' the procedure.

There are other terms for procedure used by some programmers. For example, they use the terms 'routine, 'sub-procedure' or 'subroutine'. A procedure that creates a new value is often called a function. You do not have to teach students these additional terms. However, be aware of their meaning in case they are mentioned.

## Before the lesson

The key words for this lesson are: call, procedures, random, trigger and timer event. The words are highlighted in the text the first time they appear. Their definitions are included in the Key words box at the end of the lesson. You may want to review these words before the lesson.

## ⌘ Learn about...

You will lead the first part of the lesson. Make sure students understand these ideas. You may ask them to make notes. You may use directed questioning to check understanding.

- **Event driven:** An event-driven program is one where progress is determined by actions or events. Those events may be carried out by a user (e.g. through a mouse click). An event may also be triggered by the action of another program or procedure. In this chapter the timer drives the program. The sprite moves once every second.
- **System clock:** The system clock generates a signal at regular intervals (e.g. once a second). This signal can be used to trigger an event on the screen.
- **Random:** Random numbers cannot be predicted. We use random numbers to move the sprite to a random place on the screen. Therefore, the sprite's position will be unpredictable. Being unable to predict the sprite's movements makes the game more interesting.
- **Procedures**: Explain what a procedure is. When you make a new procedure in App Inventor, it exists as a new block that you can use and reuse in your program code.

## ⏻ How to...

In the second part of the lesson students complete an exercise under your guidance. You may want to create the next part of the program on the screen, with students looking at what you do. The Student Book provides instructions.

- **Clock:** Begin work by opening the interface screen. Drag the clock object onto the interface. Wherever you put it, the clock object will move to the bottom of the screen to a section called Non-visible components. The person playing the game will not see the clock.

- **Make a procedure:** For the rest of the lesson students work on the Blocks screen. Students must find the new procedure block, give it a name, and then slot other blocks into it. In the Student Book example the procedure is called `Sprout`.

- **Random number:** Students use the random number block to make random x and y values. The upper and lower bound for these numbers will depend on the values students find.

- **Timer:** Drag the timer event onto the screen.

- **Call procedure:** Students find the new procedure they made. It should be in the purple Procedures section. Fit this block into the timer. Now the procedure will be carried out once every second.

 **Now you do it...**

Students make the app as described in the Student Book. If necessary, take more than one lesson to complete this. Ask more-confident students to start the extension activity as you support others who need help.

**What success looks like:** When students run the app they see the sprite moving at random, and changing position once a second. They demonstrate this to you.

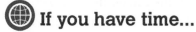 **If you have time...**

Students who complete the task can add a second moving sprite to the screen, which also moves once per second.

**What success looks like:** There are two parts to this activity.

1 Students add a second sprite to the interface (and attach a suitable image file).

2 Students add code blocks to move the second sprite at random.

There is more than one way to make this work using code blocks. Students could adapt the procedure so that it controls two sprites. The `procedure` block looks something like this (the `Timer` block would look the same).

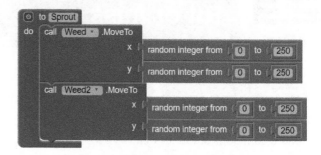

As an alternative, students create two different procedures to control the two sprites. Then they put both procedures into the code block. The `Timer` block looks something like this.

You will know students have succeeded if you look at their app and see two sprites moving at random on the screen.

 **Test yourself...**

FOUNDATION QUESTIONS

1 What is an event-driven programming language? Answer: An event-driven language is one where the code is linked to an event. When the event happens, the code is carried out.

2 What is special about a random series of numbers? Answer: A random series of numbers is unpredictable. You never know what number will come next.

EXTENSION QUESTIONS

3 When you make a procedure you have to give it a name. What else do you do? Answer: You need to add commands inside the procedure.

4 What event triggers the code in the program you made? Answer: The event is triggered by a signal from the clock (or the timer). This signal comes once every second.

## Learning outcomes

When they have completed this lesson students should be able to:

↗ use a conditional `if` structure in their code.

More-confident students will:

↗ extend their code to demonstrate understanding, working independently.

## Overview

Students have made a game with a sprite that moves at random once every second. To play the game the user touches the screen. The user tries to hit the sprite with his or her finger. In this lesson students add code to detect and count how often the user manages to touch the sprite.

This lesson uses ideas from previous books in the *Matrix* series, such as the `if` structure. Students also learn new skills, such as using touchscreen input.

## Language development

Conditional structure is the key word in this lesson. A conditional structure is a program structure that uses `if` followed by a logical test. A logical test is a test that can only have the answer 'true' or 'false'. In this example the test is: 'Has the user touched a sprite on the screen of the computer?' The user either has or has not, so the result is either 'true' or 'false'. The code is carried out if the test result is 'true'.

## ⌘ Learn about...

You will lead the first part of the lesson. Make sure students understand these ideas. You may ask them to make notes. You may use directed questioning to check understanding.

- **Touchscreen interface:** Explain that the touchscreen acts as both an input and an output device. It outputs the sprite. It detects when the user's finger touches the sprite and inputs a signal to the processor. We will call these 'hits'.

## ⏻ How to...

In the second part of the lesson students complete an exercise under your guidance. You may want to carry out this activity on screen, with students looking at what you do. Full instructions are provided in the Student Book.

- **Hit counter:** Work on the interface design. Add a label to the interface that will display the number of hits. Rename it `HitLabel`. Set the text property to `0`. There are ideas in the Student Book about further improvements to the layout.
- **Detect a hit:** Now work on the Blocks screen. Find a block that is triggered if the user touches the canvas. Next, put code inside this block.
- **`If` structure:** Find the `if` block. This should be familiar from previous books. Put the `if` block inside the `when Canvas1.Touched` block. Set the logical test as shown in the Student Book.
- **Increase value by 1:** Put code inside the `if` block so that when the user touches the sprite, the hit label text increases by 1.

## ⊕ Now you do it...

If students have followed your instructions, they will see a hit counter on the screen that shows the number of successful hits. If necessary, take more than one lesson to complete this. Ask more-confident students to start the extension activity as you support others who need help.

**What success looks like:** The completed block looks like this.

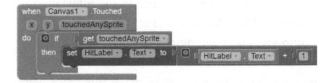

## 🌐 If you have time...

Students who complete the task early can complete a second task. They expand the interface and the code so that the game counts misses as well as hits.

**What success looks like:** Students add a second label to the interface called `MissLabel`. The completed block looks like this.

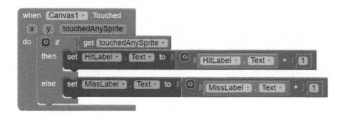

This code will work whether the user has added one or two sprites to the interface, because the code says `touchedAnySprite`.

 **Test yourself...**

FOUNDATION QUESTIONS

1 Explain why a touchscreen can be called an input and an output device. Answer: A touchscreen is an output device because it displays output for the user to look at. It is an input device because when the user touches the screen, it sends a signal in to the computer.

2 A conditional statement uses a logical test. What is the logical test used in this lesson? When is the result of the test 'true'? Answer: The logical test is 'if touched any sprite'. It is true if the user touches any sprite on the screen of the device.

EXTENSION QUESTIONS

3 How would you change this program so the hit count goes up by 5 every time you touch the sprite? Answer: The final part of the code block ends with the expression + 1 (see the image opposite). Simply change this to + 5.

4 Explain how the computer knows whether you have touched a sprite on the screen. Answer: The screen is an input device. It is sensitive to the touch. When you touch it, the screen sends a signal to the computer. It tells the computer where the user touches the screen.

For extra marks you can ask more-capable students to do Internet research into how touchscreens work. There are several types of touchscreen and it depends how much time and ability each student has. Give credit for any independent work produced.

## Learning outcomes

When they have completed this lesson students should be able to:

↗ use a timer to control events

↗ use global variables.

More-confident students will:

↗ test their app to explore its features, working independently.

## Overview

In this lesson students adjust the default value of the game timer. Adjusting the default value of the game timer means the game will go more quickly. Going faster will make the game more challenging and exciting. This gives students experience of controlling the way a program works by adjusting default values.

## Language development

'Default' is a term used in computing. A default value is what the software uses if no other value is provided by the user. In App Inventor the default value of the timer is to send a signal once every 1000 milliseconds.

In this lesson students will 'initialize' a variable. Notice that we have used the American spelling of this term. This is because App Inventor is an American program. The spelling appears as 'initialize' on the screen. In the *Matrix* series, 'initialise' is spelled using the British English form (with an 's'), unless the text specifically refers to an App Inventor initialize command.

## Before the lesson

The key words for this lesson are: default and fires. The words are highlighted in the text the first time they appear. Their definitions are included in the Key words box at the end of the lesson. You may want to review these words before the lesson.

## ⌘ Learn about...

You will lead the first part of the lesson. Make sure students understand these ideas. You may ask them to make notes. You may use directed questioning to check understanding.

- **Default value:** Explain that by changing the default value of the timer we can change the operation of the program.
- **Clock interval:** Explain why setting the clock timer to a smaller interval means the program will go faster.

## ⏻ How to...

In the second part of the lesson students complete an exercise under your guidance. You may want to carry out this activity on screen, with students looking at what you do. The Student Book gives instructions.

- **Speed up the timer:** The first activity uses the Designer screen. Find the clock object. Change the interval property from 1000 to 500.
- **Add a countdown label:** Still working on the Designer screen, add a label that will be used to show the program countdown. Set properties as shown in the Student Book.
- **Initialise the countdown:** Students used variables in *Matrix 1* and *Matrix 2*. This activity revisits that skill. The variable is called Countdown. The initial value is 60. It is a global variable.
- **Decrease by 1:** When the timer sends a signal, the sprite moves to a random location. Add another block that subtracts 1 from the value of the Countdown variable.
- **Display the countdown:** Finally, set the value of Timelabel to display the Countdown variable.

**Now you do it...**

If students have followed your instructions, they should have a program with a countdown timer. Ask more-confident students to start the extension activity as you support others who need help.

**What success looks like:** When students run the program the counter starts at 60 and counts down. After half a minute it starts to display minus numbers. This will change in Lesson 2.5.

 **If you have time...**

Students who complete the task early may start a further task. They can run tests on the app and record results.

**What success looks like:** Explanations on how to carry out tests and record them is given in *Matrix 1* and *Matrix 2*.

 **Test yourself...**

FOUNDATION QUESTIONS

**1** The Countdown variable starts with the value 60. The value for the Countdown variable goes down by 1 when the timer fires. With the default time interval, how many seconds will it take to reach the value 0? Answer: After the changes in this lesson, the timer will fire every 500 milliseconds (that is, every half a second). Therefore, after the timer has fired 60 times, that is 60 times half a second, or 30 seconds. That is the same as half a minute.

**2** If you increased the timer interval what would be the effect on your program? Answer: Students have learned that if you decrease the timer interval the game seems to go faster. Therefore, if you increase the timer interval, the game will go slower.

EXTENSION QUESTIONS

**3** When you initialise a variable what information must you provide? Answer: You must provide the name and the starting value. You must also say whether it is a local or global variable.

**4** Explain the difference between to set and get a variable value. Answer: A variable is a way of storing a value. Setting a variable puts a value into a variable. Getting the value takes the value from the variable so you can use it in your program.

---

## 2.5 Out of time

pages 52–55

### Learning outcomes

When they have completed this lesson students should be able to:
- ↗ apply the App Inventor skills they have learned
- ↗ complete an App Inventor game with a sprite moving on a canvas.

More-confident students will:
- ↗ complete further activities with minimal guidance.

## Overview

Students have made a game that counts down from 60 to 0 as users play. After it reaches 0 the countdown keeps going down, into minus numbers. In this lesson students add new commands so that the game stops when the countdown reaches 0. Students may need several lessons to complete this activity. Many students may not go past this lesson, but these students will have achieved all curriculum objectives.

# Before the lesson

The key word for this lesson is global variable. Key words are highlighted in the text the first time they appear. The definition of global variable is included in the Key words box at the end of the lesson. You may want to review this word before the lesson.

##  Learn about...

You will lead the first part of the lesson. Make sure students understand these ideas. You may ask them to make notes. You may use directed questioning to check understanding.

**Review of skills:** Review the list of skills shown here and in the Student Book. You may write the list on the board and/or lead a discussion. Encourage students to describe how they would carry out the various tasks and activities listed.

- **Use a conditional (`if... else`) structure:** The `if` block is one of the orange control blocks.
- **Make a logical test using a relational operator:** There are relational operators among the green Logic blocks and the dark blue Math blocks.
- **Put commands into a conditional structure:** The Logic block is slotted in at the top of the `if` block. Further commands are put into the body of the `if` block. If the test result is 'true' the commands are carried out.
- **Change the text property of a label:** This is done in the Interface design screen. Find the label in the Components section of this screen and click the Rename button.
- **Change the value of a variable:** Go to the orange Variable blocks. Use the `set` block.
- **Add a button to the interface:** Drag the object from the palette onto the screen.
- **Add commands that will be carried out when the user clicks the button:** Go to the Blocks screen. Find the button among the list of components in the left-hand margin. Select the component and find the `when button.click` block. Put commands into the space in this block.

##  How to...

In the second part of the lesson students complete an exercise under your guidance. You may want to carry out this activity on screen, with students looking at what you do. Or you may want to let students work independently, offering support when they get into difficulties.

- Use of the `if` block and logical test: Put an `if` block inside the `Timer` block. The commands will only be carried out if the `countdown` value is above 0. Detailed instructions are not given, but the block that students have to make is shown in full.
- Use of `if... else`: Adapt the `if` block so it includes a second `else` section. If the timer reaches 0, then `Timelabel` displays the message `TIME OUT`. The result of completing this activity is shown on page 53 of the Student Book.
- Add a Restart button to the interface. Give it suitable properties and a name.
- Add blocks to make the Restart button work. It will reset `global Countdown` to 60, and set `HitLabel` (and `MissLabel` if there is one) to 0. The result of completing this activity is shown in the '**Now you do it...**' activity.

## ⊕ Now you do it...

If students have managed to use their skills they should have produced an app that times out after 30 seconds of play. There could also be a Restart button. If necessary, take more than one lesson to complete this task. Ask more-confident students to start the extension activity as you support others who need help.

**What success looks like:** The blocks that make the game time out after 30 seconds look like this.

The blocks that make the Restart button work look like this.

## If you have time...

Students who complete the task early may start some further tasks. They may add a label to the interface that shows the number of misses; add a label that displays the percentage of hits; add code blocks so that the computer calculates the total number of touches; add code blocks so the computer calculates the percentage of hits.

**What success looks like:** The interface shows hits, misses and percentage. The actual design and layout chosen by each student may vary, but it should look something like this.

The code block to make the computer calculate and display the percentage may look like this.

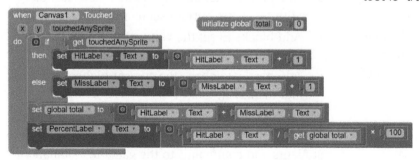

This uses a new variable called `global total`.

 ## Test yourself...

### FOUNDATION QUESTIONS

**1** The code you used in this lesson included the relational operator > (bigger than). What are the other relational operators and what do they mean? Answer: The relational operators include:

< less than

= equal

≠ not equal.

There are others but they have not been used in the *Matrix* series.

**2** Explain why the variable `Countdown` must be a global not a local variable. Answer: A global variable can be used in more than one set of blocks. `Countdown` is used in the Restart block and the Timer block.

### EXTENSION QUESTIONS

**3** Look back at the code on this page. When is `Timelabel` given the value `TIME OUT`? Answer: If `global Countdown > 0` is 'false'. In other words, when the global countdown reaches 0.

**4** When `Countdown` reaches 0 the sprite stops moving. After you hit the Restart button the sprite starts moving again. Explain in your own words why the sprite starts moving. Answer: The sprite stops moving if the result of the test `global Countdown > 0` is 'false'. It will move if the result of the test `global Countdown > 0` is 'true'. When you click the Restart button the value of `Countdown` is set to 60, so the result of the test is 'true'.

## Learning outcomes

When they have completed this lesson students should be able to:

↗ explain the difference between global and local variables.

More-confident students will:

↗ use a database to store a value

↗ get a stored value from a database and use it in their program.

## Overview

This lesson provides extra activities and features for students who have successfully completed Lessons 2.1–2.5. It does not matter if the students you teach do not reach this stage. The lesson introduces an extension concept—the use of an external database to store values when the app is not in use. Students may use this feature to store the high score for the game.

## Language development

The normal electronic memory of a computer loses its content when the power is turned off. If you want to keep a permanent record of data they must be sent to storage. 'Storage' is a general term meaning any method of retaining data that does not depend on the computer being powered. This may be the school network, a hard disk or, perhaps, flash memory.

A local variable is only used within one small part of a program—typically within a procedure. In App Inventor a local variable may only be used in a single block of code. Local variables are safer than global variables because programmers can be sure the local variable will not interfere with the rest of their code.

## Before the lesson

You may divide the class at this point. Some students may continue with previous lessons, while others work on this more advanced task. If there is a copy of the Student Book for each student, then individuals can work at their own pace.

The key words for this lesson are: local variable, storage and tag. The words are highlighted in the text the first time they appear. Their definitions are included in the Key words box at the end of the lesson. You may want to review these words before the lesson.

## ⌘ Learn about...

You will lead the first part of the lesson. Make sure students understand these ideas. You may ask students to work from the Student Book. Students should understand:

● the difference between a variable stored in electronic memory and storage on a disk drive or similar device.

● the concept of a local variable and why local variables are used by programmers.

## ⏻ How to...

In the second part of the lesson students complete an exercise under your guidance. If students are progressing well they can work directly from the Student Book, where instructions are given.

● Make sure the interface shows both hits and misses. Go back to Lesson 2.3 if it does not.

● Amend the interface to include a new section with labels for current score and high score.

● Add blocks to set the value of Score and display it.

● Add blocks to check the current highest score and display it.

## ⊕ Now you do it...

Students add commands to the game to calculate their score, display it and check whether it is the high score. Then students can play the game on the emulator or on a mobile device. They can see whether they can beat the high score.

If necessary, take more than one lesson to complete this fully. Ask more-confident students to start the extension activity as you support others who need help.

**What success looks like:** Play the game and see if it displays current score and high score. The code should resemble what is shown in the Student Book.

## If you have time...

Students who complete the '**Now you do it...** ' task early may start a final task. This is an advanced task that introduces a completely new topic. Students use an external database to store a high score value when the app is switched off.

**What success looks like:** The Student Book shows the correct code. Give credit for all independent working and effort, even if the final app is not fully functional. Students who have achieved all objectives should be proud of themselves.

 ## Test yourself...

### FOUNDATION QUESTIONS

**1** Explain what a local variable is. Answer: A local variable is one that is only used in one code block.

**2** What happens to a variable value when you close an app? Answer: The value stored in the variable is lost when the app closes.

### EXTENSION QUESTIONS

**3** What are the advantages and disadvantage of using local variables? Answer:

- Advantage: The variable is kept in a single part of the program so it cannot accidentally interfere with other blocks of code. This interference is not a problem with simple apps like the ones we have made but in large complicated apps it can be very important.

- Disadvantage: the variable can only be used in one place in the code. Many values need to be used in several different code blocks. In this case global variables must be used.

**4** Why is a stored value given a tag? Answer: Each value in the database has a tag and a value. The tag identifies the value. If you want to get the value back from the database, you identify it using the tag.

The test questions and assessment activities give you an opportunity to evaluate students' understanding. The questions are shown here with possible answers.

 ## Model answers to test questions

The test questions are based on this sample of code from an app.

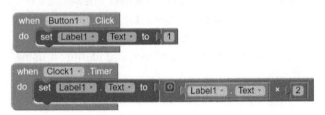

1  App Inventor is an event-driven language. What are the two events in this code? Answer: The user clicks `Button1`. The clock timer sends a signal.

2  What happens when the user clicks `Button1`? Answer: The text of `Label1` is set to the value 1.

3  What happens each time the clock timer fires? Answer: The value displayed in `Label1` doubles when the timer fires.

4  How would you change the speed of the clock timer? Answer: You would do this in the interface design screen. You would select the clock component and change the interval property.

5  If the clock timer fires once a second, what value will be shown in `Label1` after five seconds? Answer: It would show the value 32.

6  An app interface has a sprite and a canvas. What is a sprite? Answer: A sprite is an object controlled by the computer that moves on the canvas.

7  How can you send a sprite to a particular point on the canvas? Answer: You can specify the point using x and y co-ordinates.

8  When the user touches the canvas, what three pieces of information are sent to the computer? Answer: That the user has touched the canvas; the position (x and y co-ordinates); and whether the user has touched any sprite.

9  Describe the difference between a local and global variable. Answer: A local variable can only be used in one block of code. A global variable can be used anywhere in the app.

10  An event block is called: `when Screen1. Initialize`. When does this event occur? Answer: It occurs when you first start the app and the screen opens.

 ## Model answers to assessment activities

### Starter activity

All students should be able to complete this activity. Students must make an advert for the game they made. It doesn't matter how far they got through the work in this chapter.

**What success looks like:** Students make a fun advert, with screen shots from their game, and a description of its features. This does not involve any programming.

### Intermediate activity

Students add a second sprite to the app if they have not done this already. There is a description of the code required in Lesson 2.2 of this handbook. See if students can do this activity without help.

**What success looks like:** Students add a second moving sprite, which can be seen on the screen.

### Extension activity

This extension activity is only for students who complete all other work, and need extra stretch and challenge.

Students add two new buttons to the interface to set the difficulty level to beginner or expert. `ExpertButton` will make the sprite faster and smaller. `BeginnerButton` will make it larger and slower again. This means changing the sprite size and the timer interval.

**What success looks like:** The blocks of code should look something like this.

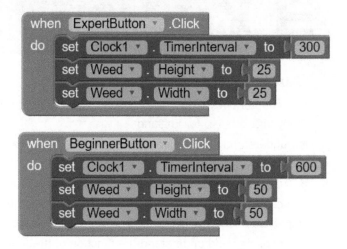

# 3 Data and the CPU

## Curriculum coverage

This chapter covers part or all of the requirements for the Computing Programme of Study (age 11–14) for England:

↗ understand simple Boolean logic (e.g. AND, OR and NOT) and some of its uses in circuits

↗ understand how instructions are stored and executed within a computer system.

This chapter also covers these main requirements for the Computing at School (CAS) Progression Pathways (for a full list of requirements met, see pages 9–10 of this handbook):

↗ recognise and understand the function of the main internal parts of basic computer architecture

↗ understand the concepts behind the fetch-execute cycle

↗ understand the von Neumann architecture in relation to the fetch-execute cycle, including how data is stored in memory

↗ understand the basic function and operation of location addressable memory

↗ understand the relationship between binary and electrical circuits, including Boolean logic.

## Preparation

There is little requirement for specialist software in this chapter. Students will need to use a spreadsheet in Lesson 3.6. The Student Book gives examples using Microsoft Excel. If your school uses a different spreadsheet, you will need to make sure the spreadsheet operates in a similar way. Students also need access to a presentation package to complete the extension activity in the review section at the end of the chapter. The Student Book does not suggest a specific presentation package.

Each 'Before the lesson' section suggests ideas for your own introductory presentations.

## Learning outcomes

By completing this chapter students will be able to:

- identify that the CPU contains switches
- explain how the CPU stores data in its memory
- understand simple Boolean logic using AND, OR and NOT logic gates
- understand that a computer uses the fetch-decode-execute cycle to process data
- explain how the CPU uses AND, OR and NOT gates to test data
- create a simple logic test using spreadsheet software
- create a simple truth table to test data.

## Let us be logical

 ## Talk about...

You can do the discussion activity offline. You could use this activity any time to vary the pace of lessons and encourage students to reflect on their learning.

It can be difficult to make topics such as Boolean logic and digital processors relevant to everyday life. They become more real and easier to understand if you can make them relevant to students' interests. Here are some more discussion ideas.

- Many companies are testing driverless cars. Would you trust a car that is driven by a computer?
- Can you think of examples of Boolean logic a computer would use when driving a car? Here is an example to get you started: IF speed limit is 30 kph AND current speed of car is > 30 kph THEN reduce speed.
- You are playing a high-definition video game with realistic characters and multiple players. You have learned that millions of switches make up a computer processor. That is all a computer can use to run programs. Can you believe that a processor built with switches can really be running your game?

- Computer processors are in many devices around the home. They control your washing machine, intruder alarm system, and your heating or air-conditioning system. Choose a device in your home. Suggest an example of an `if... then... else` statement the device's processor might use. For example, IF wash cycle = ended AND spin cycle selected = yes THEN start spin cycle ELSE stop.

## FACT

The Fact box explains that Apollo 11 made the first moon landing on 20 July 1969. Computers made sure the astronauts on board made it back to Earth safely, even though the early Apollo 11 project began without computers. Ask students whether they can imagine any activity today that does not involve computers.

## Word cloud

The Word cloud contains all the key words that are highlighted and defined in Key words boxes in the lessons. The key words for this chapter are: ALU, computer memory, registers, fetch-decode-execute, sub-routines, Boolean logic, truth table, AND statement, OR statement, AND gate, NOT gate, OR gate and IF statement.

## Learning outcomes

When they have completed this lesson students should be able to:

↗ explain how the CPU stores data in its memory.

More-confident students will:

↗ describe the difference between RAM and registers.

## Overview

In this lesson students learn about the role that a CPU plays in a computer. They learn about the four main parts of a CPU: control unit, arithmetic and logic unit, registers and clock. Students also learn about the different types of memory that a computer uses, from small registers through to large disk drives. In the first part of the lesson students revise what they learned about the input, output and storage devices of a computer system.

## Language development

In computer science we use the word 'register' to mean a small area of memory where data are recorded so that they can be accessed quickly. In the English language the word 'register' has other meanings. Schools use the word 'register' to mean a record of student attendance at classes. Most uses of the word 'register' are related to recording information. We register births and marriages in an official register. A football team can register a win or if the players are very good they might register a fifth consecutive win. We also send registered mail. The progress of a registered letter is recorded until it meets its final destination.

## Before the lesson

Can you identify any old computer equipment in your school that can be made available for demonstration purposes? Talk to your school IT technician about any old equipment you may be able to use. If there is a decommissioned computer, can you open the case to reveal the motherboard? If so, you can point out where the CPU sits. You may be able to remove a CPU and RAM chips so that students can see what these look like. If there is a decommissioned disk drive, can the case be opened so that students can see the disk and the read/write head assembly inside?

If you cannot identify real examples of equipment in your school, find images online of a CPU, RAM chips and a disk drive. Use these images to illustrate the components discussed in the lesson. You may find a suitable animation or video that demonstrates how a disk drive works on YouTube. Try a Google search, such as 'YouTube How a disk drive works'.

In the first part of the lesson students revise the knowledge they gained about the elements of a computer system in *Matrix 2*, Chapter 3, Data and the CPU. If you schedule this lesson in a computer room, students can identify whether each component in the room is an input, output or storage device. You may want to bring other devices into the room that are not normally located there. A scanner, headphones, microphone or webcam are some items you might use.

Read the Student Book to make sure you understand the content. This can be a difficult subject area for some students, as it is theoretical and, at times, abstract. You may need to provide additional support to some students to help their understanding.

The key words for this lesson are: ALU, computer memory and registers. The words are highlighted in the text the first time they appear. Their definitions are included in the Key words box at the end of the lesson. You may want to review these words before the lesson.

## ⌘ Learn about...

You will lead the first part of the lesson. Make sure students understand these ideas. You may ask them to make notes. You may use directed questioning to check understanding.

### Inside the CPU

The Student Book describes the four important parts inside the CPU.

- The **control unit** receives instructions from a program and carries them out.
- The **arithmetic and logic unit (ALU)** is the calculator inside the CPU.
- The **registers** are small areas of memory that store an instruction and the data that instruction will use.
- The **clock** is a tiny chip that sends out regular electrical pulses just like the tick of a clock.

The Student Book shows these on page 65 in a highlighted box with detailed descriptions. The Student Book also shows how the parts of the CPU fit together. Remind students of these descriptions and ask them to study the diagram, which explains how buses (wire connections that move data around quickly) connect the parts.

## Computer memory

The Student Book describes and compares the four main types of memory in a computer.

- The **registers** are small memory stores that are placed next to the CPU.
- The **cache** holds data that will be sent to the CPU in the near future.
- The **random access memory (RAM)** holds the program currently in use on a computer and the data the program is using.
- The **disk drive** stores large amounts of data permanently.

The Student Book shows these on page 66 in a highlighted box with detailed descriptions. The Student Book also uses a diagram to show how the further away memory is located from the CPU, the slower and cheaper it gets. It also shows a table listing the typical storage sizes for different types of memory. Remind students of these descriptions and ask them to study the diagram and table (on page 66).

##  How to...

There is no '**How to...**' section in this lesson, which is based in theory. However, you can carry out a class discussion as an introduction to the '**Now you do it...**' and the '**If you have time...**' activities. In the '**Now you do it...**' activity students compare the different parts of a computer memory with the way they remember things themselves. You can start a discussion by asking students to talk about a situation when they had forgotten something, perhaps an appointment or a birthday. Why did they

forget? What were the consequences of forgetting? What did they do to make sure they did not repeat the experience?

Ask students to compare the parts of a computer memory with the way they remember facts. In some cases students will simply commit facts to memory. At other times they will write things down or even store them using a computer application, such as a schedule package. If you have time, ask students to think about long-term and short-term memory. If they carry out mental arithmetic, they will remember the steps they took for a short time. By tomorrow they will have forgotten that information because they held it in their short-term memory. The computer clears its registers in a similar way. If students find themselves in a funny situation they might remember what happened for years in their long-term memory. However, they will eventually forget as the memory fades. This is similar to a computer holding information in RAM. Writing things down is like a computer storing data to a disk drive.

##  Now you do it...

Students think about the different methods they can use to remember facts. Students create a list of the various ways in which they can remember a birthday. They order the methods by the amount of time it takes to recall the information.

**What success looks like:** Students recognise that there are many ways of remembering a birthday, some of which mean they record information. They make a list of the methods, ordered from fastest to slowest.

## If you have time...

Students conduct research using the Internet to find the difference between RAM and registers in a computer.

**What success looks like:** Students use the Internet search skills they have developed elsewhere in the *Matrix* series to find sites that identify the difference between RAM and registers. Students identify several key differences, including the following.

- Registers can be accessed directly by the CPU, RAM cannot.
- Registers are built directly onto the CPU board.
- RAM contains more memory than registers.
- Registers are quicker to access than RAM.

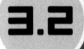 **Test yourself...**

FOUNDATION QUESTIONS

**1** List the four main parts of the CPU. Answer: Control unit, arithmetic and logic unit (ALU), registers, clock.

**2** What part of the CPU carries out calculations? Answer: The ALU carries out all calculations and logical operations.

EXTENSION QUESTIONS

**3** Why does the CPU need memory? Answer: The CPU needs memory to store the instructions that it uses, to store data temporarily while calculations take place and to store the results of calculations.

**4** Why doesn't the CPU get data directly from the computer's disk drive? Answer: It would take too long. A disk drive is much slower than the cache or RAM. The registers in the CPU are the fastest memory of all.

## 3.2 Fetch-decode-execute cycle

pages 68–71

### Learning outcomes

When they have completed this lesson students should be able to:

↗ understand that the computer uses the fetch-decode-execute cycle to process data.

More-confident students will:

↗ describe how multi-core processors can make computers operate faster.

## Overview

This lesson describes how the CPU uses the fetch-decode-execute cycle to carry out instructions. Students learn what takes place during each of the fetch, decode and execute phases of the cycle. Students also learn about different types of memory used in a computer system. They learn that the registers in a CPU are small areas of memory that can be accessed very quickly. Disk drives are slower than registers but provide more memory capacity for long-tem storage of data files.

## Before the lesson

Prepare a slide using a presentation package on the structure of the CPU diagram shown in the '**Learn about...** ' section on page 68 of the Student Book. Project the image onto the board to support a class demonstration of the fetch-decode-execute cycle during the '**How to...** ' part of this lesson. Annotating the diagram using marker pens during the lesson will support a more interactive demonstration. As an alternative, draw the CPU diagram on the board before the lesson or use a large sheet of paper.

Read the content of the '**How to...** ' section before the lesson. Your demonstration should follow the steps laid out in the Student Book so that students are prepared for the '**Now you do it...** ' activity.

The key words for this lesson are: fetch-decode-execute cycle and sub-routines. The words are highlighted in the text the first time they appear. Their definitions are included in the Key words box at the end of the lesson. You may want to review these words before the lesson.

## 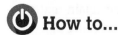 Learn about...

You will lead the first part of the lesson. Make sure students understand these ideas. You may ask them to make notes. You may use directed questioning to check understanding.

- **The CPU:** The main components of the CPU are the control unit, ALU, registers and clock. Data are loaded into the registers from cache memory and are moved around the CPU along buses.
- **Fetch-decode-execute cycle:** When an instruction is carried out it is first fetched from the cache along with any data that are needed for the instruction to be completed. The instruction is then decoded. That is, the CPU converts the instruction into a format it can use. It then stores the instruction and data in the registers. Finally, the instruction is executed by the ALU and the result is sent back to a register for storage.
- **Machine code:** The language the CPU can understand is machine code. Machine code is written entirely in binary. Any instruction must be decoded into machine code before it can be executed.

## 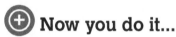 How to...

In the second part of the lesson students complete an exercise under your guidance.

This section in the Student Book provides a step-by-step demonstration of a simplified fetch-decode-execute cycle. The demonstration prepares students for the '**Now you do it...** ' activity in which pairs of students carry out a simulation. One student plays the role of the control unit and the other plays the role of the ALU. Students must understand the fetch-decode-execute cycle and the roles of the control unit and ALU during the cycle.

Run a whole-class demonstration of the fetch-decode-execute cycle to help students understand the activity's requirements. Use a diagram such as the one on page 68 of the Student Book. Prepare two simple addition instructions to demonstrate.

Demonstrate the three steps of the fetch-decode-execute cycle as detailed on pages 69 and 70 of the Student Book. Lead students through the first demonstration. Run a second demonstration using a session of questions and answers so that you can correct any misunderstanding.

## Now you do it...

Students work in pairs to run a simulation of an instruction moving through the fetch-decode-execute cycle in a CPU. One student carries out the tasks of the control unit, while the other student plays the role of the ALU. Students swap roles for a second run of the simulation.

**What success looks like:** Students demonstrate an understanding of the role of the control unit, ALU and registers. They demonstrate this understanding by correctly running a simulation of the fetch-decode-execute cycle. Each student explains what his or her role was in the simulation and identifies any improvements needed for another performance of the simulation.

## If you have time...

Students use the Internet to research what is meant by dual core and quad core processor. Students will discover why multi-core processors make computers run faster.

**What success looks like:** Students explain that a dual core processor has two CPUs working in parallel on the same chip. A quad core processor has four CPUs working in parallel. Students explain that the computer using a dual core processor runs faster than one with a single CPU. This is because, with a dual core processor, two CPUs share the work.

 **Test yourself...**

FOUNDATION QUESTIONS

**1** What is machine code? Answer: Machine code is a computer program that is written in the computer's own language, which is binary. The computer recognises some binary codes as instructions that the CPU can execute.

**2** What parts of the fetch-decode-execute cycle are performed by the ALU? The ALU performs the execute part of the cycle after the control unit has fetched from memory and decoded the data.

EXTENSION QUESTIONS

**3** Why don't programmers normally write programs in machine code? Answer: Machine code is written in the computer's language, which is binary. Binary is hard for people to understand and makes it difficult to write code and to identify where there are problems.

**4** Describe the fetch-decode-execute cycle using an everyday example, such as preparing a meal. Answer: When preparing a meal (example initial steps):

- open a recipe book and chose the recipe you are going to use (load program into RAM)
- read the first instruction—chop a medium onion (fetch)
- work out what is needed to carry out the instruction—chopping board, knife and onion (decode)
- carry out the instruction—chop the onion (execute).

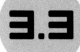

# 3.3 Arithmetic and logic

pages 72–75

## Learning outcomes

When they have completed this lesson students should be able to:

↗ identify that the CPU contains switches

↗ understand simple Boolean logic using AND

↗ create a simple truth table to test data.

More-confident students will:

↗ identify everyday events that can be expressed in Boolean logic.

## Overview

In this lesson students learn that computers are able to process logic statements as well as solve arithmetical problems. Computers can process logic because the false or true state of a Boolean logic statement is binary and can be represented by the 0 or 1 of the binary number system. Students learn how to write simple logic statements and how to lay out the statements in the form of a logic table.

## Language development

The word 'then' is an adverb that is frequently used in the English language. In logic statements 'then' is used to mean 'therefore' or 'in that case'. We might say, 'If we don't leave now, then we will be late for school'.

One of the most common uses of 'then' is when we want to say 'at that time'. We say, 'I was not available then'. A similar use for 'then' is when we want to say 'after that'. We say, 'I made a cup of tea then took it to my mother'.

## Before the lesson

Think of some examples of logic statements that you can use in your introduction to the '**How to...**' part of this lesson. Realistic logic statements can be difficult to think of quickly. Therefore, having a few already prepared will help the lesson run smoothly. The activities ask for examples from computer games or the school day. Having examples prepared from those areas will help students who are struggling to create their own examples.

The key words for this lesson are: Boolean logic and truth table. The words are highlighted in the text the first time they appear. Their definitions are included in the Key words box at the end of the lesson. You may want to review these words before the lesson.

##  Learn about...

You will lead the first part of the lesson. Make sure students understand these ideas. You may ask them to make notes. You may use directed questioning to check understanding.

- **ALU:** The ALU carries out two types of operation, arithmetic and logical. Students learned about arithmetic operations in Lesson 3.2. In this lesson students learn about logical operations. They may be less familiar with logic than the type of basic arithmetic used to demonstrate arithmetical operations in Lesson 3.2. Computer games provide an excellent source of examples of logical and arithmetical operations, which should engage students.

- **Boolean logic:** The word 'Boolean' is used in computing to describe a statement that can either be true or false. This is significant in computing because logic problems are stated in a binary form (false or true). This means logic problems can be represented by 0 or 1 in the binary number system. That explains how logic can be processed by a computer.

##  How to...

In the second part of the lesson students complete an exercise under your guidance. Prepare two or three examples you can use to demonstrate the process of defining a logic statement and creating a truth table. Use a session of questions and answers to involve students and make sure that the class understands the process. You can then move on to the '**Now you do it...**' activity.

**Now you do it...**

Students think about a computer game they play and identify two statements about the game that are logically linked. Students are given an example that they replace with a statement that reflects their own experience of a game. If students prefer, they can choose an example from any aspect of their lives. It need not be a computer game. When they have a suitable example, students combine their statements into a single logic statement and create a truth table.

**What success looks like:** Students create a realistic logic statement in which there is a clear logical relationship between the proposition and conclusion, such as 'Crossed the finish line first THEN won the race'. Students create a truth table with the proposition in the left-hand column and the conclusion in the right-hand column. The columns are correctly labelled and true/false values are correctly entered.

 **If you have time...**

In this activity students think about their school day and write three logic statements that describe events

that occur within the day, such as 'Time is 3:30 THEN go home'.

**What success looks like:** Successful students are able to analyse everyday events and write them as logic statements. The logic statements they create are clearly written and there is a link between the proposition and conclusion.

 **Test yourself...**

FOUNDATION QUESTIONS

1  What does ALU stand for? Answer: Arithmetic and logic unit.

2  Where would you find an ALU? The ALU is a part of the computer's central processing unit (CPU).

EXTENSION QUESTIONS

3  Why do we use a truth table to describe a logic problem? Answer: A truth table makes it easier to read and understand logic statements. All the possible outcomes are clearly laid out.

4  Why can we use Boolean logic with computer processors? Answer: Boolean logic can be processed by computers because the false or true value of a Boolean statement can be represented by the value 0 or 1 in binary.

# 3.4 Combining logic statements

## Learning outcomes

When they have completed this lesson students should be able to:

↗ understand simple Boolean logic using AND and OR logic gates

↗ create a truth table for a logic statement where the proposition contains either AND or OR.

More-confident students will:

↗ work independently to create a truth table.

## Overview

In this lesson students learn to write logic statements that include two parts in the proposition part of the statement. Students learn to use AND and OR operators to join two statements in the proposition. They develop skills in creating truth tables for compound logic statements.

## Before the lesson

Think of some examples of logic statements that you can use in your introduction to the '**How to...** ' part of this lesson. Realistic logic statements can be difficult to think of quickly, so having a few prepared will help the lesson run smoothly. The activities in the lesson ask for examples from computer games or the school day. Having examples prepared from those areas will help students who are struggling to create their own examples.

The key words for this lesson are: AND statement and OR statement. The words are highlighted in the text the first time they appear. Their definitions are included in the Key words box at the end of the lesson. You may want to review these words before the lesson.

##  Learn about...

You will lead the first part of the lesson. Make sure students understand these ideas. You may ask them to make notes. You may use directed questioning to check understanding.

● **Compound logic statements:** Simple logic statements are easy to write and understand, but in real life they are not very useful. Logic statements become useful when they describe situations where there is more than one factor to consider. While logic statements always have only one conclusion they can have two or more parts in the proposition.

● If there are two parts to a proposition the parts must be joined together with either an AND or an OR operator. AND is used if both statements need to be true before the conclusion is also true. OR is used if either statement needs to be true before the conclusion is also true.

##  How to...

In the second part of the lesson students complete an exercise under your guidance. Have two or three examples prepared that you can use on the board in a class demonstration. Make sure some examples use the AND operator and others use the OR operator. Students need to be clear about these areas.

● They need to understand when to use the AND operator and when to use OR. If AND is used, both statements in the proposition need to be true before the conclusion is true. If OR is used, the conclusion is true if either of the statements in the proposition is true.

● When creating a truth table, students need to ensure that they enter all combinations of false/true. In your demonstration, draw a parallel between false/true and the binary values 0 and 1. A two-part statement will always have four lines in its truth table. This becomes clear if you draw a parallel with binary. A two-digit binary number can hold four values. Those values are the binary equivalents of 0 to 3 in decimal: 00, 01, 10 and 11. If the zeros are replaced with 'false' and the ones with 'true' you have all the possible combinations for your truth table: false/false, false/true, true/false and true/true.

## Now you do it...

In this activity students work in pairs to play the game called Twenty Questions. A student thinks of the name of an object or person. The partner can ask 20 questions in order to guess the object or person.

**What success looks like:** Successful students complete the game by guessing the object or person. They recognise that they have demonstrated the use of logic to solve a practical problem.

 ## If you have time...

Students consider two examples of logic statements that describe everyday situations. They draw a truth table for each statement.

**What success looks like:** Successful students create a truth table that correctly describes both logic statements provided. The truth table for the OR statement in the first statement and the AND statement in the second statement are correctly completed. The tables are neatly laid out with a clear heading for each column.

 ## Test yourself...

FOUNDATION QUESTIONS

1  What is the missing word in this logic statement?

   Monday _____ not a holiday THEN go to school.

   Answer: AND

2  What is the missing word in this logic statement?

   Lives is zero _____ player quits THEN game over.

   Answer: OR

EXTENSION QUESTIONS

3  What is the part of a logic statement that follows THEN called? Answer: It is the conclusion.

4  If you have a logic statement with three parts to the proposition (e.g. a AND b AND c THEN d), how many possible combinations of true/false will there be? Answer: There are eight possible combinations for a three-part proposition. (Think of the problem as a three-digit binary number that has eight possible values.)

# 3.5 Logic gates

## Learning outcomes

When they have completed this lesson students should be able to:

↗ understand simple Boolean logic using AND, OR and NOT logic gates

↗ create a simple truth table to test a logic gate

↗ explain how the CPU uses AND, OR and NOT gates to test data.

More-confident students will:

↗ identify XOR, NOR and NAND gates.

## Overview

In this lesson students take their knowledge about Boolean logic and apply it to logic gates. Students find out how to recognise logic gate symbols. They also learn how to construct truth tables to describe how those gates operate.

## Language development

In the English language, a gateway is an opening in a wall or fence that allows us to pass through. A gate is a barrier that closes the opening and prevents us from passing. This can be confusing. Does a gate allow us to pass through an obstacle or prevent us from passing? The answer is that a gate allows us to pass through an obstacle if we know how to open that gate. In this lesson students discover what conditions open a logic gate in a CPU. If both inputs to an AND gate are set to 1, then the gate is opened and the output is also 1. Understanding this process is like knowing the code to a security gate.

## Before the lesson

In this lesson students apply the skills they developed in Lesson 3.4 to a new problem: logic gates. The skills they need are exactly the same. Prepare a presentation to use in your introduction to the '**How to...**' part of the lesson. Emphasise the similarity between the tasks.

Your presentation could start with the AND truth table you created for a Boolean logic statement in Lesson 3.4. As an alternative, you can prepare a slide containing a truth table similar to that on page 77 of the Student Book (the umbrella example).

A second slide could contain an image of an AND gate above the same truth table. The truth table could be modified with the original headings

crossed out and replaced with: 'input a'; 'input b' and 'output'. In the body of the table show each instance of 'false' crossed out and replaced with a 0. Also show each instance of 'true' replaced with a 1.

The key words for this lesson are: AND gate, NOT gate and OR gate. The words are highlighted in the text the first time they appear. Their definitions are included in the Key words box at the end of the lesson. You may want to review these words before the lesson.

## ⌘ Learn about...

You will lead the first part of the lesson. Make sure students understand these ideas. You may ask them to make notes. You may use directed questioning to check understanding.

- **Logic gates:** Individual switches in a CPU can be combined to make logic gates. It is logic gates that allow the CPU to perform logical operations on data.

- **Types of logic gate:** The three basic types of logic gate are AND, OR and NOT. All logic gates have just one output. All logic gates have two inputs with the exception of NOT, which only has one.

## ⏻ How to...

In the second part of the lesson students complete an exercise under your guidance.

Use the slides you prepared before the lesson to demonstrate how the truth tables students constructed in Lesson 3.4 apply to logic gates in a CPU. Emphasise how the statements in a proposition are replaced by the two inputs to an AND or OR gate. The conclusion is replaced by the output of the gate. Drawing this comparison shows that the logic gates in a computer can be used to solve everyday logic problems. Use a session of questions and answers in your demonstration to involve students and to check their understanding.

##  Now you do it...

Students draw a truth table for a NOT gate. In pairs, students then play the game called Opposites to demonstrate their understanding of the action of a NOT gate.

**What success looks like:** Students create a truth table for a NOT gate. The truth table is correctly drawn and neatly laid out. When playing the game, students demonstrate they can work together to build the longest number of opposites they can. Success in the game depends on the first student in the pair providing a prompt that has a binary response. For example, 'start' has the opposite response 'stop'.

##  If you have time...

Students use the Internet to explore three more logic gates: XOR, NOR and NAND. Students find a diagram and provide a brief explanation of what each gate does. Students also provide an everyday example of how XOR is different from OR.

**What success looks like:** Students provide a correct diagram and brief description for XOR, NOR and NAND similar to these points.

- **XOR:** This is a logic gate that will output 1 only if one or the other (not both) inputs are 1.
- **NOR:** This is a logic gate that gives the value 1 if both inputs have a value of 0. Any other combination of inputs has a value of 0.
- **NAND:** This is a logic gate that gives the value 0 if both inputs have a value of 1. Any other combination of inputs has a value of 1.

**Note:** In the case of NAND and NOR, students may say that NAND, for example, is the opposite of AND or that it is NOT AND. That is an acceptable answer. In the case of XOR, students may say that it is like OR, but where both inputs are 1 the output is 0.

An example of an XOR gate in real life is a room with two light switches. If the lights are off, flicking either of the switches will turn the lights on. Flick both and the lights stay off.

##  Test yourself...

FOUNDATION QUESTIONS

1 How many outputs do gates have? Answer: All gates have just one output.

2 If the input of a NOT gate is 0, what is the output? Answer: NOT reverses the input so if the input is 0, the output is 1.

EXTENSION QUESTIONS

3 If both inputs to an OR gate are 0, what is the output? Answer: If both inputs to an OR gate are 0 then the output is also 0.

4 Sketch the flowchart symbols for the AND, OR and NOT gates. The shapes of the three symbols have something in common. What is it and why do you think they share that feature? Answer: Students draw the AND, OR and NOT gates correctly. Refer to the Student Book pages 81 and 82 if students are unsure. What the shapes have in common is that they all have the inputs entering from the left and the output exiting to the right. Students might say they all 'point' to the right, which is correct. All gates flow to the right because the output from a gate can be the input to another gate.

# 3.6 Logic gate simulator

pages 84–87

## Learning outcomes

When they have completed this lesson students should be able to:

↗ create a simple logic test using spreadsheet software

↗ explain how the CPU uses AND, OR and NOT gates to test data.

More-confident students will:

↗ explain how the CPU uses a NAND gate to test data.

## Overview

In this lesson students learn how Boolean logic is applied in practical situations. So far students have found out how to describe real-life problems in Boolean logic. They have also discovered how to draw truth tables to show the relationship between two logical statements. In this lesson students learn how computers use logic in 'if... then... else' statements to make decisions that affect real processes. Students use a spreadsheet program to demonstrate the practical application of logic through an 'if... then... else' statement.

## Before the lesson

Students need to use a spreadsheet in this lesson. The Student Book uses Microsoft Excel for demonstration purposes. If Microsoft Excel software is available on your school network, check that students have permission to use the application before the lesson starts. If your school uses a different spreadsheet application, run through the '**How to...** ' exercise yourself and identify any differences in the way the application operates. Tell students of any differences that affect the way they will need to work to complete the lesson.

Prepare the spreadsheet that students will build in the '**How to...** ' part of the lesson. Enter a text box beneath the table created in the '**How to...** ' part of the lesson that contains an example of the formula = IF(AND(B6 = 1,C6 = 1), 1, 0). Put this formula in as large a font size as you can. Refer to this formula when you demonstrate the spreadsheet during the '**How to...** ' part of the lesson.

The key word for this lesson is: IF statement. The word is highlighted in the text the first time it appears. The definition is included in the Key words box at the end of the lesson. You may want to review the meaning of IF statement before the lesson.

##  Learn about...

You will lead the first part of the lesson. Make sure students understand these ideas. You may ask them to make notes. You may use directed questioning to check understanding.

- **'If... then... else':** This is a statement used in programming languages, spreadsheets and other application programs that support complex programming. An IF statement uses a Boolean logic test to decide between two actions. The two alternative actions are represented in the 'then' and 'else' parts of the statement. The syntax of an 'if... then... else' statement can vary. Programming languages use the words `if` before a logical test and `then` and `else` before two actions. Spreadsheet syntax replaces 'then' and 'else' with commas.

##  How to...

In the second part of the lesson students complete an exercise under your guidance.

Students complete a well-structured exercise using a spreadsheet. The Student Book uses Microsoft Excel for demonstration purposes. If students use another spreadsheet tell them if the package they are using varies from Microsoft Excel.

You may want to include a demonstration in your introduction to this section. It may be that students have some experience of using spreadsheets on other courses. You will need to judge how much detail to include in your introduction based on students' previous experience with spreadsheets. This is what you can do at the very least.

- Show students what the final spreadsheet looks like and how it works. It is important that they know what they are aiming to achieve. Seeing the finished spreadsheet will help.

- Explain the format of the IF function. Explain the three parts ('if', 'then' and 'else'). Use the formula in the demonstration as your example.
- Explain the format of the AND function. Once again, use the formula in the demonstration as your example.

## 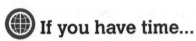 Now you do it...

Students use a spreadsheet package to create a logic gate simulator to create a truth table for an OR gate. The simulator uses an IF statement to calculate the correct outputs for two given inputs. Students model their answer on the AND gate simulator created in the 'How to... ' part of the lesson.

**What success looks like:** Students correctly create a logic gate simulator to create a truth table for an OR gate. The Student Book shows the completed OR gate truth table.

## If you have time...

Students are challenged to adapt the AND simulator they built in a spreadsheet in the 'How to... ' part of the lesson. They adapt it so that it becomes a NAND simulator. This shows that they understand how a NAND gate works. Students who carried out the extension activity in Lesson 3.5 will be prepared for this challenge.

**What success looks like:** Students adapt the AND simulator they built previously so that it simulates a NAND gate. They use the Help function in the spreadsheet to establish how to use the NOT function. Students adapt their AND spreadsheet correctly and test it. Testing requires them to draw a manual NAND truth table to check the results displayed in the spreadsheet.

##  Test yourself...

FOUNDATION QUESTIONS

**1** How would you find cell C5 in a spreadsheet? Answer: Cell C5 can be found where column C meets row 5.

**2** What tells us that an entry in a spreadsheet is a formula? Answer: A spreadsheet formula always starts with an equals sign '='.

EXTENSION QUESTIONS

**3** You used this formula in your spreadsheet: =IF(AND(B6=1,C6=1), 1, 0).
Explain what each part of the formula means.
Answer:
○ =IF: Checks if the logic statement is true or false.
○ AND(B6=1, C6=1): This is the logic statement. The statement is true if cell B6=1 and cell C6=1. Otherwise the logic statement is false.
○ ,1: This is the action taken if the logic statement is true. A 1 is entered in the cell containing the formula.
○ ,0: This is the action taken if the logic statement is false. A 0 is entered in the cell containing the formula.

**4** How does a spreadsheet simulation help us understand logic gates? Answer: A spreadsheet simulation of a logic problem allows us to enter data to test the problem. We see the outputs as we enter the input data.

The test questions and assessment activities give you an opportunity to evaluate students' understanding. The questions are shown here with possible answers.

## Model answers to test questions

1  What do the letters ALU stand for? Answer: Arithmetic and logic unit.

2  Why does the CPU need memory? Answer: The CPU needs memory to store the instruction it is currently executing and to store the data needed to carry out the instruction.

3  What is the role of the control unit in the fetch-decode-execute cycle? Answer: The control unit receives instructions from a program, decodes the instructions and carries them out. It controls all the other parts of the CPU. The control unit is the engine of the computer.

4  Where are instructions stored before being loaded into the CPU? Answer: Instructions are stored in an area of memory called the cache before being loaded to the CPU.

5  Why do we use Boolean logic with computer processors? Answer: In Boolean logic a statement can be either false or true. That can be represented in binary by 0 and 1 in the CPU.

6  How many inputs are there to the AND, OR and NOT gates? Answer: The AND and OR gates have two inputs. The NOT gate has only one input.

7  Draw a truth table for an AND gate.

| A | B | Output |
|---|---|--------|
| 0 | 0 | 0 |
| 0 | 1 | 0 |
| 1 | 0 | 0 |
| 1 | 1 | 1 |

8  Draw a truth table for an OR gate.

| A | B | Output |
|---|---|--------|
| 0 | 0 | 0 |
| 0 | 1 | 1 |
| 1 | 0 | 1 |
| 1 | 1 | 1 |

9  Describe what a NOT gate does. Answer: a NOT gate reverses the input. If the input to a NOT gate is 0 the output is 1.

10  Describe the fetch-decode-execute cycle. Answer:
   o  The control unit of the CPU fetches an instruction from the cache.
   o  The control unit decodes the instruction so that it can be processed and stores the instruction, and the data the instruction needs, in the CPU registers.
   o  The control unit instructs the ALU to execute the instruction.
   o  The ALU executes the instruction and stores any result in a register.
   o  The control unit fetches the next instruction.

## Model answers to assessment activities

### Starter activity

All students should be able to complete this activity.

Students draw a gate symbol and truth table for AND, OR and NOT gates. They use the tables to answer the questions 'When is the output 1 for each gate?' and 'How could you reverse the output for the AND gate to create a NAND gate?'

**What success looks like:** Students draw the correct gate symbol for each gate. They construct a truth table that is correct and neatly laid out. If the truth tables are correct, successful students provide these responses to the questions: 'When is the output a 1 for each gate?' Answer:

- AND gate output is 1: where both inputs a and b are 1.
- OR gate output is 1: where inputs a and b are 10, 01, or 11.
- NOT gate output is 1: where the input is 0.

'How could you reverse the output for the AND gate to create a NAND gate?' Answer: You pass the output of the AND gate to the input of a NOT gate.

### Intermediate activity

Students compare two computers, one a cheaper low-specification PC and the other a more expensive high-specification PC. Students compare several factors that influence the performance of a computer (clock speed, cache size, processor specification). Students also compare the two specifications. They highlight the factors that will make one computer perform better than the other.

Do some research before this activity to identify an online site that presents the information students are asked to identify. Pointing students to a recommended site will make the activity run smoothly.

**What success looks like:** Students identify two suitable devices to compare. They gather the information they are asked to find and lay it out clearly in a table format. Their conclusions refer to the findings in the table. Students correctly identify at least three factors that are likely to make one computer perform better than the other. Those factors include: the number of processors in the CPU (the more expensive device is likely to

have four processors, for example); clock speed is likely to be faster in the more expensive device; the more expensive device is likely to have more cache memory and more RAM. Students identify at least one general performance factor besides those they are specifically asked to identify. For example, they comment on screen specification or range of storage devices.

## Extension activity

In this activity students prepare a short presentation that explains the steps in the fetch-decode-execute cycle. The presentation format is specified in terms of the number and content of the pages.

**What success looks like:** Students create a presentation that meets the specification in termss of number of pages and the content of those pages. They demonstrate their understanding of the fetch-decode-execute cycle in a clear and concise way.

# 4  Introducing Python

## Curriculum coverage

This chapter covers part or all of the requirements for the Computing Programme of Study (age 11–14) for England:

↗ use at least two programming languages, one of which is textual, to solve a variety of computational problems

↗ design and develop modular programs that use procedures or functions

↗ create digital artefacts for a given audience.

This chapter also covers these main requirements for the Computing at School (CAS) Progression Pathways (for a full list of requirements met, see pages 9–10 of this handbook):

↗ have practical experience of a high-level textual language, including using standard libraries when programming

↗ use a range of operators and expressions (e.g. Boolean) and apply them in the context of program control

↗ select the appropriate data types

↗ define data types: real numbers and Boolean

↗ appreciate the need for, and write, custom functions including use of parameters

↗ understand and apply parameter passing

↗ apply a modular approach to error detection and correction

↗ use nested selection statements.

## Preparation

Please read the section 'Preparing to use Python' in the introduction to this handbook (page 14) before you begin this topic. Make sure you know how students can open Python and start to create programs. When using Python, students will typically have two windows open on the screen at the same time. In one window students write the program. The other window is the Python Shell, where the output of the program will appear.

This chapter assumes basic understanding of programming in general and Python in particular, derived from *Matrix 1* and *Matrix 2*. You may have students who have not completed these books. It may be best for these students to read *Matrix 1* and *Matrix 2*, Chapter 4, Introducing Python, and complete the learning activities before starting this chapter. More-able students may work quite quickly through these activities.

## Learning outcomes

By completing this chapter students will be able to:

- store a series of names as a list variable
- append an item to a list
- use a condition-controlled and a counter-controlled loop
- explain how an index number is used to identify list elements
- find the length of a list and store this value as a variable
- use code modules written by other programmers
- make and use random numbers
- store blocks of code as procedures
- define and call an procedure with a parameter
- use local variables in procedures
- write and save data as a text file.

Students will also develop their understanding of computer systems. They will be able to explain:

- how procedures help programmers to structure programs
- how the use of parameters alters the action of procedures
- how values are saved both within an app and to external storage.

## Write a program to store names

### 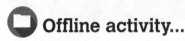 Offline activity...

The offline activity gives students a chance to do creative work without using computers. You could use this activity to introduce the six lessons in this chapter.

Students have experience in writing programs in Python. Encourage students to work together to create a Python guide for students. They can list the different Python commands they have already learned.

Creating this guide provides students with an opportunity to revisit the commands they have learned in previous years and to write out everything they can remember. Students can add to the list of commands during the six lessons, to keep a record of their learning.

###  Talk about...

The discussion is also an activity you can do offline. You could use this activity any time to vary the pace of lessons and encourage students to reflect on their learning. The discussion topic asks students to compare their experience of using App Inventor and Python.

The two languages are different. Each language presents different methods for learning programming and writing programs. Students may prefer one or the other. These are some of the points that students could make.

These are the advantages of App Inventor.

- It offers good tools to help you design a visual interface.
- It is quicker and easier to use blocks than to type commands.

- You don't have to remember text commands.
- It is easier to make a working program quickly.
- It connects directly to a mobile device.

These are the disadvantages of App Inventor.

- The programs are made of blocks and can become quite large.
- It is not like other programming languages, so you aren't learning universal skills.
- You have to do two challenging things—make the interface and then make the code.
- Using blocks is confusing for some students.

These are the advantages of Python.

- The programs are simpler and shorter.
- It feels as if you are learning a real-life programming language.
- You don't need to spend so much time designing the interface.
- You don't have to remember so many methods.

These are the disadvantages of Python.

- It is not visual.
- There is not such a colourful, lively interface.
- It does not connect to a mobile device.
- There is more use of text instead of visual elements.

## Word cloud

The Word cloud contains all the key words that are highlighted and defined in Key words boxes in the lessons. The key words for this chapter are: append, element, list, index, run-time error, code library, import, module, call, define, procedure, local variable, parameter, main memory and secondary storage.

# 4.1 Make a list

## Learning outcomes

When they have completed this lesson students should be able to:

↗ store a series of names as a list variable

↗ append items to a list

↗ use a condition-controlled loop.

More-confident students will:

↗ carry out tests to improve their understanding of the code.

## Overview

In this chapter students create a Python program that works with a list of names. They use all the Python skills they developed in previous books, and learn new skills. Each lesson builds on previous lessons. In this lesson students use the Python 'list' data structure. You can demonstrate a syntax error and show students how they can spot and correct errors by looking at error messages.

## Language development

In this lesson students make a list. A list is an example of a data structure. A data structure is a way of storing several data values, grouped together. Different programming languages have different data structures. In this chapter students use a Python data structure called a list.

This lesson introduces the term 'append'. This word means add to the end. In programming, append means to add an item of data to the end of a data structure. In this lesson students append names to a list.

## Before the lesson

Make sure Python is installed on all computers and students have access to the program. All students should have completed the Python tasks in *Matrix 1* and *Matrix 2*.

The '**How to...**' part of the lesson begins with you showing students a sample of code. Discuss the code and then students make an amended version. You may want to type up this sample code before the lesson, and simply display it when the time comes. The code is shown in the Student Book at the top of page 93.

The key words for this lesson are: append, element and list. The words are highlighted in the text the first time they appear. Their definitions are included in the Key words box at the end of the lesson. You may want to review these words before the lesson.

 ## Learn about...

You will lead the first part of the lesson. Make sure students understand these ideas. You may ask them to make notes. You may use directed questioning to check understanding.

- **List:** Students have learned that a variable stores a data value. A list is a type of variable that contains a series of values. Each value is called a list item or an element of the list.
- **Append:** Append means add an item to a list. The command is structured like this:
  - ○ type the name of the list
  - ○ then a full stop
  - ○ then the word 'append'
  - ○ the value to append is shown in brackets.
- **Syntax error:** Remind students what syntax errors are, and how error messages help us to identify them.

 ## How to...

In the second part of the lesson students complete an exercise under your guidance.

You may want to create the code on the screen, with students looking at what you do. The Student Book provides instructions.

- **Append:** Show students the example code in the Student Book and discuss it with them. Ask 'How does the user stop the loop?' (It stops when the user types anything other than Y or y.) Ask 'Why is the logical operator or used in the exit condition?' (It is used so that the user can continue the loop by typing Y or y.)

- **Variables:** Identify the three variables in the program, and where each one is initialised: (`TeamList` in the first line of code, `Another` in the second line of code, `TeamMember` in the first indented line within the `while` loop.) This is relevant later in the lesson when students look at a possible syntax error. Also talk about the data type of each variable.

- **Simplify:** In this example you make an amendment to the program. The amendment simplifies the program. However, the first example in the book has an error. Edit the code with students watching, make the deliberate mistake, and run the code to show the error message that appears. Looking at error messages and making changes is an important programming skill.

- **Correct syntax error:** The error occurs because the variable `TeamMember` is used in the header of the `while` loop, but it isn't initialised (given a value) until the line after that. The solution is to initialise the variable before the loop begins. The lines inside the loop must be swapped around too. Otherwise there will be two inputs in a row.

## ⊕ Now you do it...

Students create a program that lets them input a list of names using a loop, and then print out the complete list.

**What success looks like:** The Student Book shows the correct code. Run a student's program for yourself and check that it works in the way that it should.

## 🌐 If you have time...

Students who complete the task early may make a small amendment to the code. Then they can test the code.

**What success looks like:** The amended code will look something like this:

```
## add elements to list

TeamList = []

TeamMember = input("enter a name (leave blank to stop): ")

while TeamMember != "":
    TeamList.append(TeamMember)
    TeamMember = input("enter a name (leave blank to stop): ")

print(TeamList)
```

Notice that the `while` loop command and the prompts to the user have changed.

In testing the program, students should find no significant errors. Students should be able to add lists of various sizes, including lists with no elements and lists with many long elements.

## 📄 Test yourself...

FOUNDATION QUESTIONS

**1** What command can we use to make a list longer? Answer: `Append`.

**2** A `while` loop includes a logical test. What happens if the result of the test is 'true'? What happens if the result of the is 'false'? Answer: If the test result is 'true' the loop iterates (repeats). If the test result is 'false' the loop stops.

EXTENSION QUESTIONS

**3** The two programs in this lesson use relational operators to make logical tests. What relational operators were used in these programs? What do these operators mean? Answer:

`==` is equal to

`!=` is not equal to

**4** In this lesson you looked at two programs. Both programs add names to a list. Explain why the second program is easier to use. Answer: In the first program users have to enter two values for each iteration of the loop. They have to:

- ○ type a name
- ○ type Y if they want to continue.

In the second program users only have to enter one value, which has two purposes—if it is x the loop stops. In any other case the value is added to the list. For extension students, the empty string is used instead of the value x.

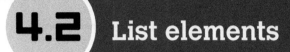

# 4.2 List elements

pages 96–99

## Learning outcomes

When they have completed this lesson students should be able to:

↗ explain how an index number is used to identify list elements

↗ find the length of a list and store this value as a variable

↗ print every element in a list by using a `for` loop.

More-confident students will:

↗ apply programming skills to solve an extra problem

↗ identify and prevent run-time errors.

## Overview

In this lesson students print out the elements of a list. They print out single elements and they print out the whole list using a counter-controlled loop.

## Language development

This lesson introduces the term 'index'. Each element in a list is called after the name of the list, plus an index (or index number).

You will use the technical term 'run-time error' in the lesson. This term has been used in *Matrix 2*. You may need to remind students of this term.

## Before the lesson

The key words for this lesson are: index and run-time error. The words are highlighted in the text the first time they appear. Their definitions are included in the Key words box at the end of the lesson. You may want to review these words before the lesson.

## ⌘ Learn about...

You will lead the first part of the lesson. Make sure students understand these ideas. You may ask them to make notes. You may use directed questioning to check understanding.

- **Elements:** Each value in a list is called an element or an item. You can work with the whole list (e.g. print out the whole list as you did in Lesson 4.1). As an alternative, you can work with a single element.

- **Index number:** Each element is identified by giving the name of the list plus an index number. The index number is shown in square brackets after the name of the list. In Python, index numbers begin at 0. Therefore, for

example, the first element of a list is list[0], the second element is list[1]. Although this numbering system may seem confusing, it helps with coding tasks. Numbering from 0 is used in many programming languages.

##  How to...

In the second part of the lesson students complete an exercise under your guidance. You may wish to create the code on the screen, with students looking at what you do. Full instructions are provided in the Student Book.

- **How many elements:** The command `len()` tells you the number of elements in a list. To use this command, put the name of the list inside the brackets

  `len(TeamList)`

This command creates a value. You can store that value as a variable and then print out the variable.

```
### how many elements in the list

HowMany = len(TeamList)
print("The team list has ",HowMany, " elements")
```

- **Print one element:** To print a single element you use the index number of the element. For example:

  `print(Teamlist[2])`

  As an alternative, the user can input a number and the computer will display the element that matches that number.

  ```
  index = input("which element do you
  want to see: ")
  index = int(index)
  print(TeamList[index])
  ```

This code will create a run-time error if the user enters a number that is too big. Remember, numbering starts at 0, so the final element of a list with five elements is `TeamList[4]`. The extension activity corrects this error.

Ask students why we convert the input to `int`. (Answer: As the input is stored as a string, and the index number is an integer, we must convert the string to integer).

- **Print all elements:** Students have learned to use the counter-variable `i` to loop up to a maximum value. Students could count through the elements of `TeamList` using this method.

  ```
  for i in range (len(TeamList):
      print(TeamList[i])
  ```

  However, Python provides an even easier way to count through the elements of a list.

  ```
  for element in TeamList:
      print(element)
  ```

  Not only is this code shorter, it is easier to read and understand. You don't have to use the word 'element' as the counter. You can use any word that helps you understand the code. For example:

  ```
  for name in TeamList:
      print(name)
  ```

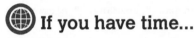 **Now you do it...**

Students create a program that prints out an individual element chosen by the user, and all the elements of the list.

**What success looks like:** The Student Book shows all the new lines of code. Run a student's program for yourself and check that it works in the way that it should.

**If you have time...**

The program code includes a potential run-time error. If the user enters an index number that is too big, then the program will crash and show an error message. Challenge your most-confident students to use `if... else` to correct this error.

**What success looks like:** Here is the code with this correction:

```
TeamList = [1,2,3]

index = input("which element do you want to see: ")
index = int(index)

if index < len(TeamList):
    print(TeamList[index])
else:
    print("number out of range")
```

If the number entered is too large then the program will print "`number out of range`".

The program will also crash if the user enters a number smaller than 0 (a negative number). This code will correct both errors.

```
TeamList = [1,2,3]

index = input("which element do you want to see: ")
index = int(index)

if index < len(TeamList) and index >= 0:
    print(TeamList[index])
else:
    print("number out of range")
```

 **Test yourself...**

The questions refer to this list:

```
CityList = ["Lima", "Athens", "Cairo",
"Madrid", "Tokyo"]
```

FOUNDATION QUESTIONS

**1** How many elements are there in this list? Answer: There are five elements in the list.

**2** Write the command to print out the first element in the list.

```
print(CityList[0])
```

**3** If you gave this command what would be printed out?

```
print(CityList[3])
```

Answer: The numbering starts at zero, so that command will print out the fourth element in the list: Madrid.

EXTENSION QUESTIONS

**4** Write the commands to print out each element in this list using a `for` loop. Answer:

```
for element in CityList:
    print(element)
```

You don't have to use the word 'element'.
For example, this code works just as well:

```
for city in CityList:
    print(city)
```

**5** If you gave this command, there would be an error. Why?

```
print(CityList[5])
```

Answer: There is no element CityList[5]. The final element of CityList is CityList[4]. Therefore, if you give this command you are asking the computer to do an impossible task and you will get a run-time error.

# 4.3 Random element

## Learning outcomes

When they have completed this lesson students should be able to:

↗ use code modules written by other programmers

↗ make and use random numbers.

More-confident students will:

↗ complete an additional programming challenge using the skills they have learned to investigate random numbers.

## Overview

In this lesson students write code to pick a name at random from a list. This feature can be useful for a teacher or team coach who needs to pick a random person to undertake a challenge (or it can be used to generate random work groups.)

Students use a module imported from a code library. Python provides a number of useful modules. These are collections of useful code created by other programmers, and made freely available for use as part of the Python download. Students use the 'random' module, which provides a range of functions that generate random numbers.

## Language development

A public library lets you borrow books and read them. A code library lets you use bits of code written by other programmers. As with public libraries, using code libraries is usually free.

A module is a collection of code that you can download from a code library. Notice that when you use a module you do not see the code in your program. However, you can use some extra commands created by the module.

'Random' is a word that many students use in day-to-day speech to mean unusual or even funny. In reality, random means something that is not predictable, and does not follow any pattern. Strictly speaking, the random numbers used in this program are pseudo-random, not quite perfectly random. However, they are near enough to random for the purpose of this task.

## Before the lesson

The key words for this lesson are: code library, import and module. The words are highlighted in the text the first time they appear. Their definitions are included in the Key words box at the end of the lesson. You may want to review these words before the lesson.

## ⌘ Learn about...

You will lead the first part of the lesson. Make sure students understand these ideas. You may ask them to make notes. You may use directed questioning to check understanding.

- **Code library:** A code library comes free with the Python download. When you install Python you gain access to the Python library of modules.
- **Module:** Each module gives you access to extra commands. For example, in this program you will import the `random` module and use it to make random integers.
- **Import:** Importing a module means adding it to your program so that you can use its features in your program.
- **Random:** A random number is one that is unpredictable. In this lesson a module called `random` is used to generate random numbers. The `random` module is available in the Python code library. To make a random number, you must give the range (the minimum and maximum values you want). In the Python `random` module the command `randint(a,b)` is used to get an integer between the values `a` and `b`.

**How to...**

In the second part of the lesson students complete an exercise under your guidance. You may want to create the code on screen, with students looking at what you do. The Student Book provides instructions.

- **Plan the code:** Take a few moments to explain the steps to make the program. First decide on the range (minimum and maximum) for the random number. Then create a number in that range. Print out the list element that matches that number.

- **Find the number range**: The range is the minimum and maximum value for the random number. You want to pick a number from the list so the minimum value is 0 (first name in the list) and the maximum value is the length of the list—1. Save these values as variables.

- **Make a random integer:** Import the `random` module and create a random integer between the minimum the maximum values.

- **Print out an element:** Print a list element, using the random number as the index.

 **Now you do it...**

Students create a program that displays a random item from a list.

**What success looks like:** The Student Book shows the complete code. Run a student's program for yourself and check that it prints out a random name.

 **If you have time...**

More-confident students have an additional programming challenge. They make a new program that generates a list of random numbers within a given range. They can then count the numbers to see whether the numbers are truly random.

**What success looks like:** This program will print 20 numbers in the range 1–10.

```
import random

for i in range(20):
    test = random.randint(1,10)
    print(test)
```

Some students may add other features to make more numbers and count up the frequency of each number, depending on their ability.

 **Test yourself...**

FOUNDATION QUESTIONS

1  What does the `randint` command do? Answer: The short answer is it makes a random number. The full answer is that it makes a random integer lying between two values—the minimum and maximum. The range of possible answers includes the minimum and maximum values.

2  The `randint` command uses two numbers. In this lesson we have called them `smallest` and `biggest`. What are these numbers for? Answer: They set the lowest and highest possible values for the random integer.

3  Write the command that will make a random number between 1 and 100. Answer:

`random.randint(1,100)`

EXTENSION QUESTIONS

4  Explain how a code library can help programmers in their work. Answer: A code library stores code modules. Programmers can import the module into their programs. Then they can use any of the commands defined in the code module. This gives programmers access to additional useful commands without having to write the code from scratch.

5  Your program includes the command `import random`. What does that mean? Answer: You have imported a module called `random` into your program. You can use any of the commands or functions included in that module.

# 4.4 Procedures

## Learning outcomes

When they have completed this lesson students should be able to:

↗ store blocks of code as procedures.

More-confident students will:

↗ work independently to simply the program by deleting additional code.

## Overview

A procedure is a stored block of code. Using procedures is central to procedural or structured programming. In this lesson students learn what procedures are and use a simple procedure to improve the formatting of the program output.

## Language development

A collection of Python commands can be stored as a procedure. A procedure can also be referred to using a range of terms, such as:

- routine
- sub-procedure
- sub-routine.

A procedure that creates a new value is often called a function.

When programmers define a procedure, they give the procedure a name. They store commands inside the procedure. Programmers can put the name of the procedure in their program ccode. The computer will carry out all the stored commands.

## Before the lesson

In the lesson you may want to show and contrast two programs:

- the program without improvements to output format
- the improved program with procedures that improve output format.

You can prepare these two versions of the program in advance. You can then run them one after the other. If this is not possible, students can refer to the example of improved output shown in the Student Book.

The key words for this lesson are: call, define and procedure. The words are highlighted in the text the

first time they appear. Their definitions are included in the Key words box at the end of the lesson. You may want to review these words before the lesson.

##  Learn about...

You will lead the first part of the lesson. Make sure students understand these ideas. You may ask them to make notes. You may use directed questioning to check understanding.

- **Procedure:** Explain what a procedure is, and how to define a procedure in our code. Procedures are found in a great many computer languages (e.g. App Inventor).
- **Call:** Explain how to call a procedure by entering its name into the code.
- **Advantages:** Procedures simplify code, making it more readable, reusable and reliable.
- **Names:** As with variables, you must choose suitable names that remind you of the job of the procedure. Remind students that in Python (and in many other programming languages) the procedure name must be followed by two brackets.

## ⏻ How to...

In the second part of the lesson students complete an exercise under your guidance. You may wish to create the code on the screen, with students looking at what you do. The Student Book provides instructions.

- **Improve:** Show and contrast the output of the original and improved program. You could discuss with students how the revised output is easier to read and better formatted.
- **Lines:** Show how to use the print command to create a line.

- **Define**: Define a procedure called `Line()` that stores this command.
- **Call**: Call the new procedure at several points in the code to improve the layout of the output.

## 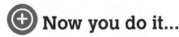 Now you do it...

Students create a program to define a procedure that draws lines on the screen.

**What success looks like:** Run a student's program for yourself and check that lines appear at several places in the output of the program. Check the listing of the program code and make sure a procedure appears near the top. The Student Book shows an example of the code on page 106.

## If you have time...

The extension activity asks students to delete rather than add code. Students must delete code leaving four actions in the program.

This tests students to make sure they understand the meaning of every bit of code in the program. The program should also include the use of the `Line()` procedure.

**What success looks like:** Here is an example of a complete program showing all these features. The student has used the `Line()` procedure, set out the code clearly, and used comments.

```
## Team List program

import random

def Line():
    print("---------------------------------")
    print("\n")

#1. Input a list

TeamList = []
TeamMember = input("enter a name (type x to stop): ")

while TeamMember != "x":
    TeamList.append(TeamMember)
    TeamMember = input("enter a name (type x to stop): ")
Line()

#2. Say how many elements there are in the list

print("Number of elements: ",len(TeamList))
Line()

#3. Print every element in the list

print("the whole list")
for element in TeamList:
    print(element)
Line()

#4. Pick a random element from the list
print("random element")
smallest = 0
largest  = len(TeamList)-1
index = random.randint(smallest,largest)
print(TeamList[index])
```

## 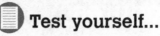 Test yourself...

This code defines a procedure:

```
def banner():
    print("* * * * * * * * * * * *")
    print("W E L C O M E")
    print("* * * * * * * * * * * *")
```

### FOUNDATION QUESTIONS

**1** What is the name of this procedure? Answer: banner.

**2** What code would you put in your program to call this procedure? Answer:

```
banner()
```

### EXTENSION QUESTIONS

**3** What would the output be if you called this procedure? Answer:

```
* * * * * * * * * * * *
W  E  L  C  O  M  E
* * * * * * * * * * * *
```

**4** What are the three advantages of using procedures in your programming? Answer: You define a procedure just once, but use it repeatedly. That is less work for you. When you know a procedure works properly, you can use it repeatedly. That means there is less chance of errors. By using sensible names for procedures you make your code easier to read.

# 4.5 Parameters

## Learning outcomes

When they have completed this lesson students should be able to:

↗ define and call a procedure with a parameter

↗ use local variables in procedures.

More-confident students will:

↗ make changes by working independently and using judgement.

## Overview

In this lesson students refine the procedure they made in the previous lesson. They use a value called a parameter to change the operation of the procedure. The lesson also revisits the concept of a local variable, which was covered in Chapter 2, App Inventor.

If students complete this lesson they have learned a lot about programming. If students do not get beyond this lesson in the time available, they have already developed good programming skills.

## Language development

This lesson introduces the technical term 'parameter'. This is a specialist technical term. A parameter is a value passed from a program to a procedure. The parameter changes the way the procedure works.

## Before the lesson

The key words for this lesson are: local variable and parameter. The words are highlighted in the text the first time they appear. Their definitions are included in the Key words box at the end of the lesson. You may want to review these words before the lesson.

##  Learn about...

You will lead the first part of the lesson. Make sure students understand these ideas. You may ask them to make notes. You may use directed questioning to check understanding.

- **Parameter:** The name of every procedure ends with two brackets. In some cases, you can put an extra value inside the brackets. This value is a parameter.
- **Local variable:** A variable that is initialised inside a program is called a local variable.

##  How to...

In the second part of the lesson students complete an exercise under your guidance. You may want to create the code on the screen, with students looking at what you do. Full instructions are provided in the Student Book.

- **A procedure called `Title()`:** Show students how to make a procedure that does only one thing. In this case, the procedure is called `Title()`. What is the disadvantage of this?
- **Use a parameter:** To use a parameter we need to do two things. First we change the way the procedure is defined, then the way it is called from the main program. Show students how to change the definition of the procedure. In the Student Book the parameter is called `anytext`. This is to emphasise that the parameter will work with any text value.
- **Call with parameter:** We can call the procedure using parameters. Whatever parameter we put in the brackets will affect what is output by the procedure.
- **Use a local variable:** Show how a variable inside the procedure (a local variable) can be used to change the way the procedure works. This section of the lesson also introduces a new Python technique. You can use the multiplication symbol to 'multiply' a string (print that string lots of times).

```
print("="*12)
```

## ⊕ Now you do it...

Students create a program that uses a new procedure called `Title` to show text in title format. This will improve the appearance of students' program output.

**What success looks like:** The top of the students' program may look something like this. The two procedures are defined. This student has used the * symbol to 'multiply' the number of '-' characters in the output string.

```
### working with lists

import random

## procedures

def Line():
    print("-"*25)
    print("\n")

def Title(anytext):
    print(anytext)
    length = len(anytext)
    print("=" * length)
```

When you run the program the output may look something like this. Of course the exact names and wording may be different.

```
enter a name: Jordan
enter a name: Zara
enter a name: Leanne
enter a name: Jatinder
enter a name: x
-------------------------


Size of team
=============

the team has  4  members
-------------------------


Members of team
=============

here are all the team members
Jordan
Zara
Leanne
Jatinder
-------------------------


Random name
=============

here is a random name
Zara
```

 **If you have time...**

The extension activity challenges students to make a change that is not shown in the Student Book. If they succeed in this the `Title()` procedure will look like this.

```
def Title(anytext):
    print(anytext.upper())
    length = len(anytext)
    print("=" * length)
```

The output of the program will look something like this (this is an extract from the full output).

```
MEMBERS OF TEAM
===============

here are all the team members
Jenni
Maria
Hiba
Lakshmi
Angelique
-------------------------
```

**Test yourself...**

This code defines a procedure:

```
def Line(symbol):
    print(symbol * 12)
```

FOUNDATION QUESTIONS

1 What is the name of this procedure? Answer: `Line()`

2 What is the name of the parameter used in the procedure? Answer: `symbol`.

EXTENSION QUESTIONS

3 If you entered this code, what would the output be? `Line("@")`

Answer: `@@@@@@@@@@@@`

4 What code would you enter to see a line of 12 question marks? Answer: `Line("?")`

# 4.6 Save the list

## Learning outcomes

When they have completed this lesson students should be able to:

↗ write and save data as a text file.

More-confident students will:

↗ write an additional program that reads a stored data file.

## Overview

By the time students reach this lesson they will have learned a lot about programming. This lesson provides an extra stretch and challenge for students who are confident and able. Do not force the pace with students who may not reach this final lesson.

Students save `TeamList` as a stored text file. Students already save their programs. For example, they use the school network or local storage. They will use this same storage area. The **'If you have time…'** activity will encourage students who are working with confidence to write a completely new program that reads the stored text file.

## Language development

This lesson introduces the term 'main memory'. The main memory of the computer is the active electronic memory, which stores data as electronic signals. The contents of main memory are lost when the computer is switched off. Secondary storage is permanent storage that is not lost when the computer is switched off.

## Before the lesson

The key words for this lesson are: main memory and secondary storage. The words are highlighted in the text the first time they appear. Their definitions are included in the Key words box at the end of the lesson. You may want to review these words before the lesson.

## ⌘ Learn about…

You will lead the first part of the lesson. Make sure students understand these ideas. You may ask them to make notes. You may use directed questioning to check understanding.

● **Saving values:** Students may have realised they need to type in the team members' names each time they run the program. This provides a clear

illustration of how normal computer memory does not retain its contents when the program is closed.

● **Storage locations:** Secondary storage retains its contents. Review the storage locations available to students (e.g. memory stick, hard disk, school network storage). What storage location do students use to store their Python programs?

## ⏻ How to…

In the second part of the lesson students complete an exercise under your guidance. You may wish to create the code on the screen, with students looking at what you do.

● **Open text file:** Show students how to open a new text file for writing. (At this stage the file will have no content.)

● **Write to the file:** Demonstrate how to save a piece of text to the file. The example in the Student Book saves the words 'Test data'. Students can save any text they like. Show students how to find the file with this content in their storage area. If they open the file they will see the saved text.

● **Save the list:** Now students can write each name from the list to the text file. Once again, after running the program, check storage to find the stored file.

● **Separate lines:** Finally, by adding a line break, students produce a well-structured and formatted file, which saves their work.

## ⊕ Now you do it…

Students create a program that writes the list of team members to a stored text file.

**What success looks like:** Look at a student's code. You should see additional lines at the bottom of the program that look like this.

```
### save the data

with open("teamlist.txt", "w") as openfile:
    for element in TeamList:
        openfile.write(element+"\n")
```

In the storage area you will find a file called teamlist.txt. If you open the file, it looks like this. Of course the names will be different.

```
teamlist - Notepad
File  Edit  Format  View  Help
Andy
Rhianne
Janghir
Salman
Dov
```

If you see this code and the resulting file the student has succeeded.

## 🌐 If you have time...

The extension activity will take a long time. By following the Student Book instructions, confident and capable students create a completely new Python program. The new program reads the stored text file and displays the contents on the screen.

**What success looks like:** The complete new program looks something like this:

```
## program to read a text file

with open("teamlist.txt") as openfile:
    data = openfile.read()

print("text from file")
print(data)

data = data.strip()
data = data.split("\n")
print("text turned into a list")
print(data)
```

If you run the new program the output on the screen looks something like this:

```
text from file
Andy
Rhianne
Janghir
Salman
Dov

text turned into a list
['Andy', 'Rhianne', 'Janghir', 'Salman', 'Dov']
```

If you see the code and the output, the student has succeeded.

##  Test yourself...

This test refers to this short Python program.

```
testdata = "Rainbow"
with open("password.txt", "w") as openfile:
        openfile.write(testdata)
```

FOUNDATION QUESTIONS

1  What is the name of the string variable in this program? Answer: `testdata`

2  This code writes data to a text file. What is the name of the text file? Answer:
   `password.txt`

EXTENSION QUESTIONS

3  If you opened the file what text would you see in the file? Answer: `Rainbow`

4  Explain the difference between electronic memory and permanent storage. Answer: Use your judgement to award marks for understanding. Give credit for answers that explain these points.
   ○  The data created when you use software are stored in electronic memory.
   ○  The contents of electronic memory are lost when the computer is turned off.
   ○  Permanent storage does not require electricity.
   ○  The contents of external storage are not lost when the computer is switched off.
   ○  We can use permanent storage to retain data when we are not running the software. That means we don't have to type the data in again.

The test questions and assessment activities give you an opportunity to evaluate students' understanding. The questions are shown here with possible answers.

##  Model answers to test questions

**1** Write the command to initialise an empty list called Metals. Answer:

```
Metals = []
```

**2** Write the command to append "gold" to Metals. Answer:

```
Metals.append("gold")
```

**3** A user appended several elements to Metals. Write code to find the number of elements in Metals and print out this number. Answer:

```
number = len(Metals)
print("The number of elements in
the list: ", number)
```

**4** Write the command to print out the first element in Metals. Answer:

```
print(Metals[0])
```

Note that the first element in a list has the index number 0 not 1.

**5** Write the code that would print out all the elements in Metals using a `for` loop. Answer:

```
for element in Metals:
        print(element)
```

Note that students can give the counter variable any name. This example uses the name `element`. Other names would work just as well, for example:

```
for item in Metals:
        print(item)
```

**6** What is a code library? Answer: A code library is a stored collection of program code modules. You can use the stored code in your own programs, which saves time and reduces errors.

**7** What does it mean to import a module to your program? Answer: You can use the commands from the module in your own program.

**8** What are the advantages of using procedures in programs? Answer: You define a procedure just once, but use it repeatedly. That is less work for you. When you know a procedure works properly, you can use it repeatedly. That means there is less chance of errors. By using sensible names for procedures you make your code easier to read.

**9** How do you call a procedure? Answer: You enter the name of the procedure into your code, followed by open and closed brackets.

**10** What is a parameter? Answer: It is a value you add when you call a procedure. It changes the way the procedure works.

## 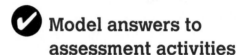 Model answers to assessment activities

### Starter activity

All students should be able to complete this activity. Students enter the currency program as shown in the Student Book and then add two further lines.

**What success looks like:** The completed program should look like this.

```
## currency program

currencylist = ["Euro", "Dollar", "Pound", "Yen"]
currencylist.append("Rupee")
currencylist.append("Peso")
print(currencylist)
```

Run the program to make sure it works. The output should look something like this.

```
["Euro", "Dollar", "Pound", "Yen",
"Rupee", "Peso",]
```

## Intermediate activity

Students add a loop structure to append a series of values to the list. To help students, you might give them the names of additional currencies to add. Some examples are:

- Franc
- Krone
- Real
- Yuan Renminbi
- Dinar
- Forint
- Baht.

**What success looks like:** The completed code will look something like this. The output will be an extended list with multiple added items.

```
## currency program

currencylist = ["Euro", "Dollar", "Pound", "Yen"]
currencylist.append("Rupee")
currencylist.append("Peso")

newcurrency = input("enter a new currency (type x to stop): ")

while newcurrency !="x":
    currencylist.append(newcurrency)
    newcurrency = input("enter a new currency (type x to stop): ")

print(currencylist)
```

## Extension activity

Students are challenged to write a program that allows the user to add or delete currencies and then save the result as a text file. There are many ways to achieve this result. The example shown here uses a short menu to allow the user to choose whether to add or delete.

Very able students could improve this program by checking whether a currency is already present on the list before adding or deleting it.

- If a currency is already present it should not be added.
- If a currency is not present it cannot be deleted.

**What success looks like:** The program should look something like this.

```
## currency program

currencylist = []

choice = input("enter A to add, D to delete, X to exit: ")

while choice !="X":
    currency = input("enter the name of the currency: ")
    if choice == "A":
        currencylist.append(currency)
    if choice == "D":
        currencylist.remove(currency)
    choice = input("enter A to add, D to delete, X to exit: ")

print(currencylist)

with open("currency.txt", "w") as openfile:
    for currency in currencylist:
        openfile.write(currency)
```

# 5 Information Technology

## Curriculum coverage

This chapter covers part or all of the requirements for the Computing Programme of Study (age 11–14) for England:

↗ understand how data of various types (including text, sounds and pictures) can be represented and manipulated digitally, in the form of binary digits.

This chapter also covers these main requirements for the Computing at School (CAS) Progression Pathways (for a full list of requirements met, see pages 9–10 of this handbook):

↗ understand how bit patterns represent numbers and images

↗ understand how numbers, images, sounds and character sets use the same bit patterns

↗ understand the relationship between resolution and colour depth, including the effect on file size

↗ know the relationship between data representation and data quality.

CAS extension:

↗ understand the client-server model, including how dynamic web pages use server-side scripting and that web servers process and store data entered by users.

## Learning outcomes

In this chapter students learn how computers use binary data to represent text, images and sound. Students find out about the factors that affect the quality of images and audio data files. They discover that increasing the quality of a file also increases its size. Students learn about compression techniques that allow the size of large media files to be reduced to save storage space and improve the speed of transmission over networks. In the final lesson students develop their skills so they can secure their data with strong passwords.

By completing this chapter students will be able to:

• explain how the file size of an image is related to the resolution and colour depth

• explain how file compression can reduce the size of image files

• describe lossy and lossless compression

• name different image file types and how to use them

• describe how compression can affect the quality of an image

• describe how a computer saves audio as binary data

• explain how the quality of an audio sample is related to sampling rate and bit depth

• explain how text is stored as binary by using ASCII code

• explain how numbers, images, sounds and characters use the same bit patterns

• recognise the difference between a static and a dynamic web page

• explain why encryption is used to protect data on the Internet

• create strong passwords.

## The changing web

###  Talk about...

The discussion is an activity you can do offline. You could use this activity any time to vary the pace of lessons and encourage students to reflect on their learning. The discussion topic is about how the Internet has changed how we access and listen to music. The way in which we pay for music has also changed. Many people no longer purchase music on a CD or vinyl record. There are many issues around how we pay for music and the extent of piracy and copyright.

Here are further discussion points you can use.

- Many people use the Internet as their main source of news. News affects our opinions and the way we act. How can you make sure that the news you get from the Internet is reliable and honest?

- There are over 6,000,000,000 Google searches carried out every day. Can you trust a Google search to provide accurate and reliable information?

- Has the Internet made us more or less vulnerable to the actions of criminals?

- In recent years, several serious cyber attacks have shut down large parts of the Internet. How would having the entire Internet shut down for a week affect you?

## FACT

The Fact box in this chapter presents numbers that show how important the Internet has become in daily life. Individuals and organisations depend on the Internet to:

- get information and news
- communicate with friends, family and colleagues
- buy and sell goods and services
- manage business and finance
- store personal and business information.

The Internet has grown rapidly from the early 1990s when the World Wide Web was invented. This has been positive for the most part. However, the rapid and uncontrolled growth of such an important resource raises many issues and questions. The 'Talk about...' activity highlights questions you can discuss with students. You will also find topical news items about the Internet that raise questions about how the Internet is changing our lives for better or worse. Discussions around issues raised in the news can be interesting and valuable to students.

## Word cloud

The Word cloud contains all the key words that are highlighted and defined in Key words boxes in the lessons. The key words for this chapter are: colour depth, image resolution, compression, compression ratio, lossless compression, lossy compression, analogue signal, bit depth, sampling, sampling rate, formatted text, client-side script, encryption and server-side script.

## 5.1 Measuring images

pages 120–123

### Learning outcomes

When they have completed this lesson students should be able to:

↗ explain how the file size of an image is related to the resolution

↗ explain how the file size of an image is related to colour depth.

More-confident students will:

↗ recognise that the actual size of an image file is significantly smaller than the expected file size, based on the number of pixels it contains and its colour depth.

## Overview

In this lesson students learn about the effect of resolution and colour depth on an image. The quality of an image is directly related to the resolution and colour depth of that image. A high image resolution and colour depth also increases the size of an image file. This is because it takes more data to create a high-quality image, such as a full-colour photograph. Students learn how to identify the resolution and colour depth of an image by investigating image properties.

## Language development

The word 'resolution' has several meanings in the English language. In chemistry, resolution means to break something down into its parts—a chemical compound, for example. This meaning leads to the use of resolution in this lesson. The resolution of a scientific instrument, such as a telescope, is the smallest unit that the instrument can measure. When talking about digital image resolution, the smallest unit is a pixel.

## Before the lesson

Students need to access the Internet to find an image to investigate. If this is not possible, make several images available to students in a shared folder on your school network. Select a variety of images ranging from icons to full-colour pictures so that students can choose one that appeals to them.

The **'How to…'** section of the Student Book uses examples that are based on using Microsoft Windows. If your school uses a different operating system check before the lesson how image properties are displayed. If it is not how they are displayed using Microsoft Windows, highlight the differences in your introduction to the lesson.

The key words for this lesson are: colour depth and image resolution. The words are highlighted in the text the first time they appear. Their definitions are included in the Key words box at the end of the lesson. You may want to review these words before the lesson.

## ⌘ Learn about...

You will lead the first part of the lesson. Make sure students understand these ideas. You may ask them to make notes. You may use directed questioning to check understanding.

- **Image resolution:** This is the number of pixels that are used to make up an image. The more pixels that are used, the higher the quality of the image. The size of an image is usually stated as horizontal and vertical dimensions in pixels. For example, an image might be 200 pixels × 300 pixels. A file with these dimensions will contain 60,000 pixels (200 × 300).

- **Colour depth:** Each pixel in an image is a single colour. A picture is more realistic if it uses more colours. Each colour in a digital image is represented by a unique binary code. If a single byte is used to store colour information, 256 colours can be stored. This is because there are only 256 unique binary codes available in a single byte. More colours can be stored if more bytes are used to store colour information. The 24-bit true colour system uses three bytes. There are over 16,000,000 unique binary codes available in 3 bytes, so the number of colours that can be stored is much higher than using one byte.

- **Image file size:** High-quality images create larger image files than low-quality images. This is because the image resolution and colour depth of the image are higher in a high-quality image than in a low-quality image.

##  How to...

In the second part of the lesson students complete an exercise under your guidance.

This part of the lesson asks students to use several skills to find, save and view the properties of an image. Some students will be more confident with the demands of this exercise than others.

You can demonstrate how to:

- enter a search string into a browser to find a source of Creative Commons free-to-use images
- select an image and save it to your network drive—demonstrate how to create a new folder to store the image
- show how to find the image using the operating system file browser
- show how to right-click to open the image Properties box
- point out the tabs in the Properties box so that students know they need to use the tabs to find the information required.

## Now you do it...

Students search the Internet to find a suitable image. Once they have found one they look at the image properties and make a table of the properties that are most relevant to image resolution and colour depth.

**What success looks like:** Students are able to identify images with a Creative Commons licence that allows free use of the image. They successfully download an image and save it. They find the image in a file browser and look at the file properties. Students find specific information about the file. They correctly work out the image resolution and colour depth of the image.

## If you have time...

Students use the information they gathered in the 'Now you do it...' activity to calculate an expected file size. They calculate the expected file size by multiplying the number of pixels in the image by colour depth. Students compare the actual file size to the expected file size. To do this, they must convert actual and expected file sizes into the same units of memory (e.g. megabytes). Once they have carried out the conversion, students calculate actual file size as a percentage of expected file size.

**What success looks like:** Students choose the correct data to calculate expected file size. This is the number of pixels in the image multiplied by the colour depth of the image (probably three bytes). Students convert the expected file size into the same unit of measurement as the actual file size. They accurately calculate the size of the actual file as a percentage of the expected file size.

## Test yourself...

FOUNDATION QUESTIONS

1  Why is 24-bit true colour better than 256-colour for storing a photo? Answer: 24-bit true colour can store nearly 17,000,000 colours—many more than 256-colour. A colour photo needs many colours if it is to look realistic.

2  How many bytes are needed to store a pixel in a 24-bit image? Answer: Three. There are eight bits in a byte. 24 divided by 8 is 3 bytes.

EXTENSION QUESTIONS

3  Why is a true-colour image file larger than a 256-colour image file of the same size? Answer: It takes three bytes to store the colour information for each pixel in a true-colour image compared with only one byte in 256-colour.

4  How many pixels are in a file with dimensions of 100 × 200 pixels? Answer: 20,000 pixels.

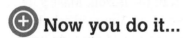

# 5.2 Compressing images

## Learning outcomes

When they have completed this lesson students should be able to:

↗ explain how file compression can reduce the size of image files.

More-confident students will:

↗ demonstrate how compression reduces the size of digital image files.

## Overview

In this lesson students find out how compression makes image files smaller. Large files can be a problem in computing. A large file takes up space on a disk drive. It can also take a long time to download a large file over the Internet. Computer scientists are always looking for better ways to make files smaller without reducing the quality of the images.

## Language development

In everyday English language, 'compress' means to reduce the size of an object by applying pressure to it. When we compress something, we apply a force to make it smaller. When we say we have compressed a data file, we mean we are making the file smaller. In the case of data, we do not apply force to the file. We apply an algorithm that alters the form of the data stored in a file so that it takes less space.

## Before the lesson

Read the text in the Student Book so that you understand the methods of compression described in the **'How to…'** section. Prepare an image on a 5 × 5 grid that you can use as an example in your introduction to the **'How to…'** part of the lesson. Do not make the image too complicated. Ensure that there are plenty of repeating colours in the grid. A simple design will allow you to complete your demonstration quickly. It will also provide a significant compression ratio.

The key words for this lesson are: compression and compression ratio. The words are highlighted in the text the first time they appear. Their definitions are included in the Key words box at the end of the lesson. You may want to review these words before the lesson.

## ⌘ Learn about...

You will lead the first part of the lesson. Make sure students understand these ideas. You may ask them to make notes. You may use directed questioning to check understanding.

- **Compression:** Almost all graphic formats use some form of compression to reduce the size of the file. It is important that students understand why image files are compressed. Graphic files can be large. It is important that the files are as small as possible so they can be transmitted as quickly as possible across the Internet. Smaller image files also reduce the amount of disk space required to store them. The Student Book outlines the principles of two methods of compression. Compression is a complex subject, so the methods described are simplified. The Student Book describes the methods in a practical way that can be demonstrated using images created manually on a grid.
  - ○ **Method 1** uses the lowest binary values to represent the most frequently used colours in the images. Therefore, if black is the most frequently used colour in an image it is represented by a single digit: 0. In a 24-bit colour image this method saves 23 bits of storage space for each black pixel.
  - ○ **Method 2** recognises that some colours are repeated in adjacent pixels in an image. In this method a repeating colour is represented by two values: the first value represents the colour and the second value tells the computer how many times to repeat that colour.

**How to...**

In the second part of the lesson students complete an exercise under your guidance. Use the image you prepared in the 'Before the lesson' section to demonstrate the two compression methods described in the Student Book. Show students that both methods will lead to a smaller file size than if they save each colour as a single one-byte binary number. If you are short of time, demonstrate compression by coding just one or two lines of the image.

Make sure the image you use is simple and has plenty of repeating colours. Using a simple design with repeating colours is especially important when illustrating method 2. Use this opportunity to tell students that they should also use a simple design with repeating colours when they carry out the 'Now you do it...' activity.

 **Now you do it...**

Students work in pairs to create a three-colour design on a 5 × 5 pixel grid. Once the design is created, students convert the design into a set of instructions using the compression technique shown in the Student Book. When students have completed their instructions they pass them to a partner, who attempts to reconstruct the design.

**What success looks like:** Students demonstrate that they understand the principles of image compression by accurately coding and decoding a simple image. When coding the image, students create a neat, well-organised set of instructions. When decoding their partner's instructions, students work logically from top-left to bottom-right of the grid to reconstruct the image.

 **If you have time...**

Students create a new design on a 5 × 5 pixel grid. You could suggest that they use three colours in their new design. If time is short, ask students to

use the design they created in the 'Now you do it...' activity. If you do this, change the pairings so students are not familiar with each other's design. In this activity students use the same compression technique as in the 'Now you do it...' activity. However, they write the code as binary. After reconstructing their partner's image, students calculate the image's compressed file size. In the final part of the activity students calculate the compressed file size as a percentage of estimated file size (25 bytes).

**What success looks like:** Students demonstrate that they understand binary data representation by coding and decoding images represented as binary numbers. Students correctly calculate the compression ratio of their partner's image.

 **Test yourself...**

FOUNDATION QUESTIONS

**1** Why is a compressed file stored in binary? Answer: A compressed image file is a digital file stored and processed on a computer. All digital files are stored in binary.

**2** Where would you look to find the actual size of an image file? Answer: The size of a file is shown in the file's Properties window.

EXTENSION QUESTIONS

**3** An uncompressed 80-byte image file is compressed to 60 bytes. What is the compression ratio? Answer: The compression ratio is the size of the compressed file shown as a percentage of the uncompressed file size. In this case it is 60 ÷ 80 × 100 = 75%.

**4** What size is an uncompressed file that has 100 × 50 pixels and uses eight-bit colour? Answer: The file contains 5,000 pixels. Each pixel needs one byte to store the colour information. The uncompressed file is 5,000 bytes or 5 kilobytes.

# 5.3 Squishing images

pages 128–131

## Learning outcomes

When they have completed this lesson students should be able to:

↗ describe lossy and lossless compression

↗ describe how compression can affect the quality of an image

↗ name common image file types and how to use them.

More-confident students will:

↗ explain why different image file types result in different file sizes for the same image.

## Overview

In this lesson students learn about data compression as it is used in image files. They use a graphics application to save files in various formats, and demonstrate that compression can make a significant difference to file size. Students also demonstrate that lossy compression can lead to a loss of image quality.

## Before the lesson

Students need to use a graphics application package for this lesson. The Student Book uses a web-based application to demonstrate how to compare file sizes: Pixlr (`pixlr.com/editor`). Check that Pixlr can be accessed through a browser across your school network.

If Pixlr is available, use it to open an image file and carry out the '**How to…**' exercise and the '**Now you do it…**' activity. If Pixlr is not available across your network or you choose not to use it, ensure that another graphics application package is available. Using Pixlr is helpful because it allows adjustment of JPEG format quality through a simple slider. Pixlr also previews file size without needing to save the file. Your chosen graphics application must have both these functions. The application should also support saving JPEG, BMP and PNG format images. If the alternative application does not preview file size, students will have to save each format and compare the different file sizes through the operating system file browser.

The lesson activities assume that students already have a suitable image saved from a previous lesson to work on. Make an image available on a shared network drive for any students who do not have an image. Choose an image with high contrast areas and some clear diagonal lines.

The key words for this lesson are: lossless compression and lossy compression. The words are highlighted in the text the first time they appear. Their definitions are included in the Key words box at the end of the lesson. You may want to review these words before the lesson.

##  Learn about…

You will lead the first part of the lesson. Make sure students understand these ideas. You may ask them to make notes. You may use directed questioning to check understanding.

- **Importance of file size:** Keeping file size low is important because smaller files save file space and take less time to download over the Internet.

- **Lossless compression:** Most image file formats use lossless compression algorithms. That means the algorithms achieve compression without reducing the quality of an image. PNG is an example of lossless compression.

- **Lossy compression:** This compression technique allows image quality to be reduced in order to create smaller files. JPEG is an example of lossy compression. Most images on Internet pages are saved in JPEG format.

##  How to…

In the second part of the lesson students complete an exercise under your guidance.

In your introduction to this part of the lesson demonstrate how to open an image in Pixlr. Show students how to save a file and how to change the file format in the Save dialogue box. For JPEG files, show how the quality can be varied. Show students where they can see the file size preview. Emphasise that there is no need to save files.

**Now you do it...**

Students explore the effect that reducing the quality of a JPEG file has on file size. Students record and compare file sizes for a range of compression ratios using the same image. Students also observe and report on the effect of a high level of compression on the quality of an image.

**What success looks like:** Students demonstrate that using higher levels of compression in a JPEG file leads to smaller file size. Students record file size at three or four levels of compression for the same image. They note the results in table form. Students compress and save a file before comparing the quality of the image with the original pixilation, particularly in diagonal lines. They may also notice a halo effect, though the intensity of the halo will depend on the image they have chosen.

 **If you have time...**

Students compare file size for the same image saved in three different formats: PNG, BMP and JPEG (80 per cent quality). Students note the file sizes and explain the differences based on what they have learned in this lesson.

**What success looks like:** Students record the results of their observations clearly, for example in a table. The results show varying file sizes for the same image stored in three file formats. The results show that the BMP format results in the largest file size and JPEG the smallest. In explaining the differences in file size, students mention that JPEG is the smallest file size because it uses lossy compression. They may also say that the JPEG

format can be further reduced in size. Students note that the BMP is the largest file because BMP does not use compression. Exceptional students provide some measure of the comparison between the file sizes. They may say, for example, that the BMP file is 300 per cent larger than the JPEG file.

 **Test yourself...**

FOUNDATION QUESTIONS

**1** Give an example of a file type that supports lossy compression. Answer: JPEG (JPG) is the most common file format that supports lossy compression.

**2** Give an example of a file type that supports lossless compression. Answer: GIF and PNG are the two lossless file types named in the Student Book. There are many more examples and if students give an answer other than JPEG they are probably correct, though you will need to check if you are unsure.

EXTENSION QUESTIONS

**3** Why would you use JPEG images in a web page? Answer: JPEG supports lossy compression. That means you can choose to reduce the quality of the image to achieve a smaller file. That is important on web pages that contain images because you want the page to download as quickly as possible.

**4** Why might you use a PNG file if you were attaching an image to an email to send to a friend? Answer: PNG is a lossless file format. That is, any compression used will not reduce the quality of the image. You use a lossless format when you want the image your friend receives to be the same high quality as the one you have on your computer.

# 5.4 Sample the music

## Learning outcomes

When they have completed this lesson students should be able to:

↗ describe how a computer saves audio as binary data

↗ explain how the quality of an audio sample is related to sampling rate and bit depth

↗ explain how text is stored as binary by using ASCII code.

More-confident students will:

↗ explain the difference between analogue and digital sound.

## Overview

In this lesson students learn how computers use ASCII code to allow letters, numbers and other keyboard characters to be stored as binary numbers. Students also learn how sound is recorded digitally so that it can be stored and processed by a computer.

## Language development

One of the most common modern uses of the word 'sample' is to describe capturing a piece of sound to be included in a music recording. The sound captured is often from a well-known recording by another artist. Students may already know this specific use of the word and may become confused to see the Student Book using 'sample' differently. The Student Book uses the word in a technical sense.

A sample is a small amount of something that shows what the whole thing is like. Scientists take samples for analysis. Statisticians take samples of opinion to predict how a whole population will think or act. In this lesson the word 'sampling' is used in the same sense. A computer takes tiny fragments of sound at short time intervals and uses them to recreate analogue music.

## Before the lesson

Students will use a text editor in this lesson. The Student Book uses Microsoft Notepad to demonstrate the **'How to...'** part of the lesson. Before the lesson, check whether Microsoft Notepad is available to students across your school network. Using an alternative text editor will not present any significant challenge. If you are using an alternative to Microsoft Notepad, identify any differences in the way your package operates. Highlight the differences in your introduction to the **'How to...'** part of the lesson.

Prepare two slides to demonstrate how computers store text and sound in binary. On one slide have a table that shows all or part of the ASCII code table. You can find a code table using an Internet search. On the other slide create an image similar to that on page 133 of the Student Book.

You may be able to find a video or animation to make your introduction more dynamic. Searching for 'Bit depth and sample depth explained' using YouTube will return some results that you may find helpful.

The key words for this lesson are: analogue signal, bit depth, sampling and sampling rate. The words are highlighted in the text the first time they appear. Their definitions are included in the Key words box at the end of the lesson. You may want to review these words before the lesson.

## ⌘ Learn about...

You will lead the first part of the lesson. Make sure students understand these ideas. You may ask them to make notes. You may use directed questioning to check understanding.

- **Storing text in binary:** ASCII code is used to translate between characters that people can understand and a binary code that computers can understand. Where more characters are needed to support languages other than English, Unicode can be used instead of ASCII. ASCII is part of Unicode, which can store the characters needed to support hundreds of languages.

- **Storing audio in binary:** In the real world, audio is a continuous signal that is constantly changing. We call this continuous audio an analogue signal. Computers cannot store analogue data. To store audio, a computer samples an analogue audio signal. The computer collects data at frequent intervals. The computer takes the samples so frequently that when the digital signals are turned back into sound, it seems to be continuous. The frequency with which the computer takes the samples is called the sampling rate. A high sampling rate gives high-quality digital audio. However, it also creates large files.

The quality of an audio file also depends on how much data are stored each time a sample is taken. The more data that are stored for each sample, the higher the quality of the audio and the larger the file size.

 ## How to...

In the second part of the lesson students complete an exercise under your guidance. As an introduction to this part of the lesson you may want to demonstrate how the ASCII table can be used to translate keyboard characters into binary codes, which can be stored and processed by the computer. You may also want to display a copy of the ASCII table on the board and challenge students to translate letters and short words to and from binary.

Use a diagram such as the one in the Student Book (page 133) to explain the process of sampling an audio signal. Use a session of questions and answers to check that students understand the idea of sampling and sampling rate. It may be useful to emphasise the similarities between sampling rate and image resolution. Both increase the number of 'elements' in a digital file and so increase the detail. You can make another useful comparison between bit depth in image and sound files. In both cases a higher bit depth uses more bytes to store more detailed information for each element in a file.

 ## Now you do it...

Students create a small text file and estimate the size of the file by counting the number of characters in it. They examine the properties of the saved file and compare the actual file size with their estimate.

**What success looks like:** Students use a range of skills to demonstrate that an ASCII character takes one byte of storage. These skills include using a text editor, using the operating system's file browser and looking at a file's properties.

 ## If you have time...

Students research using the Internet to discover the difference between music recordings that are stored digitally and on vinyl. They consider the advantages and disadvantages of digital recording over vinyl. They also consider why the popularity of vinyl has lasted over time.

**What success looks like:**

1   What is the difference between a recording on a vinyl record and a recording on a CD? Answer: A vinyl record is an analogue recording while a CD recording is digital. An analogue recording is a made in a continuous groove of a vinyl disc. The computer makes a digital audio file by sampling the original analogue sound and recording it. The computer does this many times per second to produce the final version.

2   Why do some people prefer vinyl records to CDs or MP3s? Answer: There are several reasons why people prefer vinyl. Some say that an analogue sound can only be recreated properly by an analogue recording. Others say that an analogue sound is 'warmer' or just 'better'. A third reason is that people want to hear a recording as it was meant to be heard.

3   Are there any advantages of CDs and MP3s over vinyl records? Answer: A digital recording cannot be scratched or wear out. The devices that play digital recordings are portable and can be played anywhere. Digital recordings can be streamed or downloaded over the Internet. Digital recordings don't take much physical space to store.

 ## Test yourself...

### FOUNDATION QUESTIONS

**1**   What is ASCII code used for in computing? Answer: The ASCII code contains a list of keyboard characters, each one alongside a binary number. The code is used to convert from characters that people can read into a binary number that the computer can process.

**2**   How does increasing the bit depth of an audio sample affect file size? Answer: Increasing bit depth makes the file larger. Increasing bit depth uses more bytes to store information about a sound. That means a more detailed representation of a sound can be saved. Increasing the bit depth of an audio sample is similar to increasing the colour depth in an image.

### EXTENSION QUESTIONS

**3**   How does increasing the sampling rate affect the audio quality? Answer: Increasing the sampling rate improves the audio quality. If the sampling rate is increased, the computer measures the sound more often. Increasing the sampling rate in audio is similar to increasing the number of pixels in an image.

**4**   If a text file contains 12,000 characters including spaces, what will the file size be? Answer: 12 kilobytes (that is, 12,000 bytes).

# 5.5 What is a byte used for?

pages 136–139

## Learning outcomes

When they have completed this lesson students should be able to:

↗ explain how numbers, images, sounds and character sets use the same bit patterns.

More-confident students will:

↗ explain that some data stored in files are to be used by an application program.

## Overview

In this lesson students learn that the same binary codes can be used to represent text, image, sound and other types of data, such as formatting instructions. They learn that the meaning of a piece of binary data is decided by its context. For example, a byte of data in a JPEG file represents colour information, while the same code in a text file represents an ASCII character.

## Before the lesson

Students will use a word processor and text editor in this lesson. The Student Book uses Microsoft Word to demonstrate the '**How to…**' part of the lesson. Before the lesson, check whether Microsoft Word is available to students across your school network. Using an alternative word processor will not present any significant challenge. Check how the word count function operates in the alternative word processor. If the word count function displays the number of characters including spaces in a file, then students will have no problems. Run through the '**How to…**' and the '**Now you do it…**' activity before the lesson. If you are using an alternative to Microsoft Word, identify any differences in the way your package operates. Highlight the differences in your introduction to the '**How to…**' part of the lesson.

The key words for this lesson are: formatted text. The words are highlighted in the text the first time they appear. Their definitions are included in the Key words box at the end of the lesson. You may want to review these words before the lesson.

##  Learn about…

You will lead the first part of the lesson. Make sure students understand these ideas. You may ask them to make notes. You may use directed questioning to check understanding.

- What can a byte store? A byte stores eight binary digits. However, what do those digits mean? Students have seen that a byte can represent an ASCII character. A byte can also represent colour information in an image file, or a fragment of sound in an audio file. It can also represent part of a program instruction or a formatting instruction. A byte can represent many things.
- How does the computer know whether 00110101 is a character, a colour or an instruction? The computer does not know. Only when the data are loaded into an application does the meaning become clear.

##  How to…

In the second part of the lesson students complete an exercise under your guidance. In your introduction to this part of the lesson demonstrate how students should use the word count function. Students need to use the operating system's file browser and access a file's properties in the '**Now you do it…**' activity. If you feel it is necessary, remind students how to find files and view a file's properties.

##  Now you do it...

Students create a word processor file containing two or three sentences. They use the word count function to count the number of characters in the document. Students compare the actual file size with the number of bytes needed to store only the characters. They calculate how much larger the word processor file is than a text file containing the same number of characters. This activity is similar to the one using a text file in Lesson 5.4. The activity will demonstrate that a word processor stores additional formatting data, which a text editor does not need.

**What success looks like:** Students use a range of skills to demonstrate that a word processor stores considerably more data than the characters it contains. A word processor contains formatting. The skills students develop include using a word processor to create a file, using the word count function, using the operating system's file browser and looking at a file's properties.

## If you have time...

Students open a word processor file in a text editor and explore what they see. The Student Book guides them to think about what they see in the file. However, the questions are open-ended.

**What success looks like:** Students note the amount of data in the file they have opened. The file contains many pages of characters, few of which are readable. The text contained in the word processor file may or may not be visible in the text file. Text is generally not visible in a Microsoft Word file. Students may interpret not being able to see the text as a security measure. Students should be able to find some text in the file that gives clues to the formatting being used and give examples.

##  Test yourself...

FOUNDATION QUESTIONS

**1** Why is a word processor file bigger than a text file that contains the same number of characters? Answer: The word processor file contains data for the characters used in a document, but it also contains codes that tell the word processor how to format the characters. For example, some characters may be in bold or italic. A text file contains only the characters and no formatting information.

**2** If the byte 01101000 appears in a text file what type of data will it represent? Answer: Every byte in a text file represents a character. That character might be a letter, number or special character, such as a question mark. In ASCII code, 01101000 represents the letter 'h', but it is not necessary for students to know this.

EXTENSION QUESTIONS

**3** If the byte 01101000 appears in a PNG file what type of data will it represent? Answer: A PNG file is an image file. A byte in a PNG file will usually contain data instructing the computer what colour to display a pixel in the image.

**4** Why do you need to count spaces when working out how much memory a piece of text will use? Answer: A space is an ASCII character so it needs to be stored in binary like any other character.

# 5.6 Keeping data safe

## Learning outcomes

When they have completed this lesson students should be able to:

↗ recognise the difference between a static and a dynamic web page

↗ explain why encryption is used to protect data on the Internet

↗ create strong passwords.

More-confident students will:

↗ learn how to assess the strength of passwords.

## Overview

In this lesson students learn that scripts are used to create dynamic websites. Scripts are used to deliver up-to-date information to many of the sites we use on the web. Security is a growing concern, as sending personal information across the Internet has become common practice for many. Students learn that secure passwords are vital to protect personal and financial data on the Internet. They learn how to create and manage passwords to ensure that their data are as secure as possible.

## Before the lesson

The key words for this lesson are: client-side script, encryption and server-side script. The words are highlighted in the text the first time they appear. Their definitions are included in the Key words box at the end of the lesson. You may want to review these words before the lesson.

## ⌘ Learn about...

You will lead the first part of the lesson. Make sure students understand these ideas. You may ask them to make notes. You may use directed questioning to check understanding.

- **Static and dynamic websites:** In the early days of the Internet all websites were static, with information that did not change. All the information on a page was coded in HTML. To update the information, the page had to be edited by hand. Editing information in this way took a long time and the page could contain out-of-date information. Many modern websites are dynamic. Web pages contain instructions that automatically fetch content from a database, ensuring that content is always up to date. Showing up-to-date information is important for news and e-commerce sites.

- **Scripts:** Web pages can contain scripts that perform actions, such as retrieving data from a database. There are client-side scripts and server-side scripts. The two types of script work together to provide services that allow users to shop online and pay for goods, for example.

- **Encryption:** When data are sent over the Internet they are often encrypted so that they cannot be read if they are intercepted.

- **Passwords:** Passwords to protect our data online need to be secure. Organisations that handle sensitive data, such as banks, create websites with especially strong security. This level of security can include multiple levels of passwords.

## ⏻ How to...

In the second part of the lesson students complete an exercise under your guidance. Read the **'How to...'** section in the Student Book and make sure you understand the technique of creating strong passwords. In your introduction to this part of the lesson show students how to create a secure and memorable password. This will prepare students for the **'Now you do it...'** activity.

## ⊕ Now you do it...

Students use the technique described in the Student Book to create secure passwords that they can remember.

**What success looks like:** Students create three secure passwords and retain two for their own use. They become confident in using this technique.

**If you have time...**

Students use a web service designed to test the strength of passwords. This will assess the passwords students created in the '**Now you do it...**' activity.

**What success looks like:** Students use the website to check that the passwords they have created are secure.

**Test yourself...**

FOUNDATION QUESTIONS

**1** What is the minimum number of characters you should use in a password? Answer: Eight.

**2** Why should you change your password regularly? Answer: You should change your password regularly to protect yourself in case someone else has discovered it.

EXTENSION QUESTIONS

**3** Explain the difference between a static and dynamic website. Answer: A static website has all the content coded in HTML on its web pages. A dynamic website gets some of its data from a database. A web page on the dynamic site will contain instructions that fetch up-to-date information from a database to display on the web page.

**4** List three things you can do to make sure your passwords are secure. Answer: Use eight characters or more; use a mix of letters, numbers and other characters in the password; change passwords regularly; use different passwords for different sites; avoid dictionary words and personal information that people might guess; do not write a password down or reveal it to anyone.

The test questions and assessment activities give you an opportunity to evaluate students' understanding. The questions are shown here with possible answers.

## Model answers to test questions

1 What is a byte? Answer: A byte is the basic unit of memory used by a computer. It is made up of eight binary digits (bits).

2 How many bytes are needed to store a single pixel in a 32-bit colour image? Answer: Four bytes (32 bits ÷ 8).

3 What do we mean by the resolution of a digital image? Answer: The resolution of an image is the number of pixels that are used to make up the image.

4 Why does the quality of a digital image improve if the colour depth increases? Answer: If colour depth increases, more bits are used to store the colour information about a single pixel. That means that more colours can be used to make up the image.

5 Why is a PNG file described as a lossless format? Answer: PNG is a lossless compression format. Lossless is a method of compression used to make the image file smaller without reducing the quality of the image.

6 JPEG provides lossy compression. What does that allow someone saving a file to do? Answer: Lossy compression allows the person saving the file to reduce the quality of the image in order to get a much smaller file size.

7 What method does a computer use to convert analogue audio sounds into digital data? Answer: The computer uses sampling to convert analogue sound into a digital audio file.

8 List two ways that you can improve the quality of a digital audio recording. Answer: The quality of a digital audio file can be improved by increasing the sample rate. That is, the number of samples taken per second is increased. The quality of a digital audio file can be improved by increasing the bit depth. That is, the number of bits used to store information about each sample is increased.

9 How does the sampling rate affect the size of an audio file? Answer: A higher sampling rate increases the size of an audio file.

10 Explain the difference between a static and a dynamic website. Answer: A static website is one where the content is coded onto each web page in HTML. The information does not change until the page is edited. A dynamic website gets some of its content from databases. That information can be updated regularly without editing the website.

## Model answers to assessment activities

### Starter activity

All students should be able to complete this activity.

Students create an information sheet that provides guidance on keeping data secure by setting strong passwords and managing them effectively. The information sheet will be accompanied by a step-by-step guide to creating a strong password.

**What success looks like:** Students create an information sheet that highlights three positive actions ('Do… ') and three negative actions ('Don't… ') that other students should take to protect their data through passwords. These are achievable and effective. Students also give a clear and concise set of instructions for creating a secure password. Both sheets are clearly laid out using a word-processing application.

### Intermediate activity

Students find three Creative Commons free-to-use images to illustrate the information sheet they produced in the starter activity. They compress the images before inserting them into the information sheet.

**What success looks like:** Students use an appropriate search string in an Internet search to find Creative Commons free-to-use images on the Internet. They select three images relevant to their sheet and insert them into the word-processed document. They resize the images and enter the images into the document in an appropriate position.

Before using the images, students have converted them to JPEG format (if necessary). They have also adjusted the quality of the image to produce a smaller file size. The compressed images they produce should remain at an acceptable quality with no pixelation visible.

## Extension activity

Students use the information and images they included in the information sheet they produced in the intermediate activity. They create a presentation entitled 'Using strong passwords'. The target audience is other students who are given login details for your school network for the first time.

**What success looks like:** Students produce a clear, concise presentation that delivers practical guidelines on how to create and manage personal passwords in an engaging way. The presentation has a heading page, and two further pages communicating the advice headed 'Do… ' and 'Don't… ' that students have already written.

## Curriculum coverage

This chapter covers part or all of the requirements for the Computing Programme of Study (age 11–14) for England:

- ↗ undertake creative projects that involve selecting, using, and combining multiple applications to achieve challenging goals
- ↗ create digital artefacts for a given audience
- ↗ meet the needs of known users with attention to trustworthiness, design and usability
- ↗ resuse, revise and re-purpose digital artefacts for a given audience.

This chapter also covers these main requirements for the Computing at School (CAS) Progression Pathways (for a full list of requirements met, see pages 9–10 of this handbook):

- ↗ recognise ethical issues surrounding the application of information technology beyond school
- ↗ identify and explain how the use of technology can impact on society
- ↗ design criteria for users to evaluate the quality of solutions, use the feedback from the users to identify improvements and make appropriate refinements to the solution
- ↗ effectively design and create digital artefacts for a wider or remote audience
- ↗ document user feedback, the improvements identified and the refinements made to the solution.

CAS extension:

- ↗ explain and justify how the use of technology impacts on society, from the perspective of social, economic, political, legal, ethical and moral issues.

## Preparation

This chapter uses Google Docs to encourage students to collaborate. Review the activities in each lesson so that you are aware of how Google Docs will be used throughout the chapter. Lesson 6.1 covers the different ways in which technology has had an impact on our lives. One way is in the ability to collaborate and work remotely. You might want to investigate local businesses to see if any use technology in this way. A presentation from a local business on how the company uses technology for collaboration and remote working could be helpful to students.

## Learning outcomes

In this chapter students consider how technology has changed how we live our lives. Technology has had an impact on the way we work, the way we communicate, the way we buy and sell products and the way we entertain ourselves. In the world of work, technology has made it easier for us to collaborate with teams wherever the team members are located in the world. Students use collaborative tools to explore how technology can help in the planning, creation and evaluation of documents and products.

By completing this chapter students will be able to:

- explain how technology has changed the ways in which we live and work
- explain copyright, plagiarism and software piracy
- explain the difference between bitmap and vector images
- create a simple graphic of their own
- create a report using a template
- share, edit and add comments to a document online
- create a simple slideshow
- understand peer assessment and self-assessment
- explain the difference between quantitative and qualitative data
- create an online form.

# Information technology in everyday life

 **Talk about...**

You can do the discussion activity offline. You could use this activity any time to vary the pace of lessons and encourage students to reflect on their learning. The discussion has two parts.

The first question asks students to try to predict how technology will change their lives over the next ten years. In your introduction to the discussion, point out some trends that could have an impact on the ways in which we live our lives. One issue to raise is the impact of technology on employment. For example, will self-driving cars replace taxi drivers? 3D printing could create a revolution in the way we buy goods. If we need a replacement part for a car or washing machine, we may, in future, download a design that we can print at home rather than ordering a physical part. That development not only changes the way we shop but it also has huge implications for the manufacturing and distribution sectors.

The second question asks students to think about what life would be like without computers. You could download videos and pictures of the world of work before the computer age. For example, an Internet search using 'typing pool' will produce images showing the number of people, mostly women, involved. Computers have replaced nearly all of these jobs. Today, software can generate letters automatically and even send them to the recipient.

## FACT

The Fact box highlights that there are over 120,000,000 accounts registered to use Google Drive, with the number growing every day. Students will use Google Docs software and collaborate using Google Drive. What is the potential for working in wider groups? What are the risks in having so much information stored by a single organisation, such as Google? How has the Internet grown at such a pace in just 25 to 30 years? How much further can it grow? Has the Internet grown equally everywhere in the world and with every part of society? If not, is that fair?

## Word cloud

The Word cloud contains all the key words that are highlighted and defined in Key words boxes in the lessons. The key words for this chapter are: collaborative technology, e-commerce, online banking, copyright, plagiarism, software piracy, graphics software, vector images, comment boxes, template, presentation software, peer assessment and self-assessment.

# 6.1 The impact of information technology

## Learning outcomes

When they have completed this lesson students should be able to:

↗ explain how technology has changed the ways in which we live and work.

More-confident students will:

↗ create a Google Docs document.

## Overview

In this lesson students find out some of the ways in which the Internet has changed our lives. Students discover the impact that the Internet has had on the way we buy and sell things, the way we work and the way we entertain ourselves. Students explore some of the facilities that collaborative technologies, such as Google Docs, provide.

## Language development

Since the invention of the Internet many words in the English language have a new form. Where we once had learning, mail and commerce we now also have e-learning, e-mail and e-commerce. The 'e' stands for electronic. Adding 'e' to a word usually means that the activity takes place over the Internet instead of face to face.

## Before the lesson

Students need to open a Google Docs account. This is an important activity because they will use Google Docs (`www.google.com/docs/about/`) throughout the chapter. They will use Google Docs to explore collaborative working and the tools that are available to support collaboration online.

Make sure students can access Google Docs over your school network. If there are any issues, work with the school technician to resolve them. If you are unfamiliar with Google Docs, create an account yourself and follow the walk-through so that you can support students.

The key words for this lesson are: collaborative technology, e-commerce and online banking. The words are highlighted in the text the first time they appear. Their definitions are included in the Key words box at the end of the lesson. You may want to review these words before the lesson.

##  Learn about...

You will lead the first part of the lesson. Make sure students understand these ideas. You may ask them to make notes. You may use directed questioning to check understanding.

- **Technology and money:** The Student Book covers two aspects of technology and money. The first is managing a personal bank account online. The second is paying for goods at a point of sale using contactless payment. Students are unlikely to have much personal experience of online banking; you might try to find suitable video presentations to help with this part of the lesson. Search YouTube using a search string such as 'online banking demonstration' or 'how does online banking work?' You should find a demonstration that you feel meets the needs of students.

- **Technology and shopping:** Students are more likely to have experience of shopping online than they have of e-banking or collaborative working. Use a session of questions and answers to explore students' experiences of e-shopping. Is online shopping something they enjoy? Perhaps they prefer visiting a shopping centre. Have students had any particularly good or bad experiences of shopping online?

- **Technology and entertainment:** The Student Book covers two main aspects of technology and entertainment. The first is how digital media has changed how we watch TV and listen to music. The second is how social media is changing the ways in which communicate with friends and family. Students should have personal experience to contribute to a class discussion.

- **Technology and the workplace:** This section addresses how technologies, such as video conferencing, e-mail and collaborative tools, can support remote working. Does your school have any links with local businesses? If so, do any of those businesses use technology to support remote working? A presentation by someone from a local business who can describe how the company uses and benefits from technology and collaborative working would be helpful. Could that presentation be made via a video conference link?

##  How to...

In the second part of the lesson students complete an exercise under your guidance. Students need to set up a Google Docs account in this lesson. Students use Google Docs extensively in activities throughout this chapter. Use your introduction to this part of the lesson to demonstrate the process of accessing the Google Docs site and setting up an account.

## 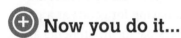 Now you do it...

Students open Google Docs in a browser window and register a user account. Students view the site walk-through to learn what functions Google Docs offers.

**What success looks like:** Students create a Google Docs account and show a basic understanding of the services the site offers.

## 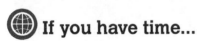 If you have time...

Students navigate the Google Docs website.

**What success looks like:** Students create and save a Google Docs document.

## 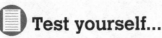 Test yourself...

### FOUNDATION QUESTIONS

1  Define e-commerce and give an example. Answer: E-commerce is buying and selling goods over the Internet. Examples of well known e-commerce sites include Amazon, eBay and iTunes. Most large stores now have Internet sites they use for e-commerce.

2  What is near field communication? Answer: Near field communication is technology that lets devices use wireless communication over a short range. This is used in contactless payment systems, for example.

### EXTENSION QUESTIONS

3  What is teleworking and how do you think it can help employees? Answer: Teleworking is using the Internet to work remotely. The Internet allows workers to connect to their office network from home or from another remote location. Connecting to the office network allows a teleworker to use files and software and keep in touch with colleagues.

4  Give an example of a third-party payment company and explain how third-party payments work. Answer: PayPal is an example of a third-party payment company. A third-party payment company provides a secure service for people (e.g. buyers and sellers) to make and receive payments. Both buyer and seller must have an account with the third-party payment company. When a buyer and seller agree a sale, the seller records the details in his or her account. The buyer pays for the goods into the third-party account. The third-party payment company passes the money from the buyer to the seller.

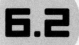

## 6.2 Using technology responsibly

pages 152–155

### Learning outcomes

When they have completed this lesson students should be able to:

↗ explain copyright

↗ explain plagiarism

↗ explain software piracy.

## Overview

In this lesson students find out about the use of copyright to protect intellectual property. They discover the dangers of breaking copyright law through plagiarism and piracy. Students learn steps they can take to ensure that they have permission to use the work of others.

## Language development

Plagiarism has only one meaning in the English language. It means taking the ideas or work of others and passing them off as your own. Plagiarism has become associated with the Internet, perhaps because people think that easy access to information and the ability to 'cut and paste' encourage plagiarism. However, the word 'plagiarism' is an ancient one. It was first used in English in the 17th century. The word has origins in Latin and ancient Greek. Plagarius in Latin means kidnapper!

## Before the lesson

Students need to search the Internet to find examples of media that they can download and freely use under a copyright agreement or Creative Commons licence. Check before the lesson that students have access to the Internet and can download media files. Check that students will be able to download audio files. Establish whether downloading large MP3 files is practical across your school network.

While some students will find suitable resources to download with no problems, others may find it more difficult. Identify one or two sources of Creative Commons licensed resources yourself that you can share with students, where necessary. Try the search string 'Creative commons image library' to locate suitable images. Flickr is a site that has a large collection of Creative Commons images:
`https://www.flickr.com/creativecommons/`

The key words for this lesson are: copyright, plagiarism and software piracy. The words are highlighted in the text the first time they appear. Their definitions are included in the Key words box at the end of the lesson. You may want to review these words before the lesson.

 ## Learn about...

You will lead the first part of the lesson. Make sure students understand these ideas. You may ask them to make notes. You may use directed questioning to check understanding.

● **Copyright:** This is the legal protection of intellectual or creative property. Students must recognise that they have a responsibility to use the content they find on the Internet or elsewhere responsibly. Creative Commons licences provide a way of identifying how content can be used.

● **Trademarks and patents:** A trademark protects the branding of companies and other organisations. Patents provide protection for inventions.

● **Plagiarism:** This happens when a person uses work that was created by someone else and claims it is his or her own. Take this opportunity to discuss the need for students to reference the work of others used in assignments.

● **Software piracy:** This is the illegal copying or distribution of software. Anyone using unofficial sites to download computer games or music is breaking the law.

 ## How to...

In the second part of the lesson students complete an exercise under your guidance.

In your introduction to this part of the lesson demonstrate how to search the Internet for free-to-use Creative Commons images and other resources.

The Creative Commons site (`https://creativecommons.org/`) is a useful resource. Use this site to demonstrate how content owners can add Creative Commons licences to their work. An Internet search for 'Creative Commons images' will give students an idea of how many resources are available to them under licence. Flickr has a useful Creative Commons page that uses icons to show the permissions granted to particular images (`https://www.flickr.com/creativecommons/`).

 ## Now you do it...

Students use the Internet to find sources of copyright-free items that they can use in creating a presentation.

**What success looks like:** Students identify and download three pieces of media: an image, a piece of music and a piece of written work. For each piece of work, students correctly identify why they have permission to use the material. They explain the conditions under which the material can be used. Students present their findings in a format of their choice. Students might use a presentation package to include audio media in their presentation. However, it isn't necessary for them to do this for the purposes of this activity.

 ## If you have time...

Students carry out Internet research on copyright and plagiarism. They create a poster identifying useful facts about copyright and plagiarism to share with the class.

**What success looks like:** Students create an informative poster, which clearly explains copyright and plagiarism.

 ## Test yourself...

### FOUNDATION QUESTIONS

**1** Give three examples of work that could be protected by copyright. Answer: There are many possible answers. Copyright could cover any original work (e.g. an image, a poem, a report or a fiction book).

**2** What could happen if you were found to plagiarise something? Answer: Committing plagiarism can lead to prosecution for breaking copyright law. Students who plagiarise work in assignments can have their work disqualified from assessment. A student who plagiarises work may fail a course or be asked to do the work again.

### EXTENSION QUESTIONS

**3** How is copyright different from a trademark? Answer: Copyright protects the intellectual property rights of the person who created a piece of work. A trademark protects the branding of a company or other organisation.

**4** Explain ways in which copyright might be broken. Answer: Copyright can be broken if a work such as a book or piece of music is downloaded illegally. Copyright can also be broken if work is copied or used without permission.

# 6.3 Creating graphics in Google Docs  pages 156–159

## Learning outcomes

When they have completed this lesson students should be able to:

↗ explain the difference between bitmap and vector images

↗ create a simple graphic of their own.

More-confident students will:

↗ modify an existing image file.

## Overview

In this lesson students find out about the difference between bitmap and vector images. Students will learn about the functions that are commonly available in a graphics package. They will use a graphics package to create and modify images.

## Language development

'Vector' is a mathematical term. It describes two points in terms of the direction and magnitude between them. For example, point B is 6 centimetres from point A at 45 degrees. The word 'vector' is used in computing for vector graphics. A vector graphic is saved as a list of instructions that describe how the computer should draw an image by moving from one point to another on a page.

## Before the lesson

Students need to use Google Docs in this lesson. Make sure it is available across your school network. Students need to register a user account for Google Docs. They should have registered in Lesson 6.1.

In the '**Now you do it...**' activity students will use the Google Docs graphics application to modify images. Students should have an image available from the '**Now you do it...**' activity in Lesson 6.2. Make a suitable image available in a shared folder for students who do not have one.

The key words for this lesson are: graphics software and vector images. The words are highlighted in the text the first time they appear. Their definitions are included in the Key words box at the end of the lesson. You may want to review these words before the lesson.

## ⌘ Learn about...

You will lead the first part of the lesson. Make sure students understand these ideas. You may ask them to make notes. You may use directed questioning to check understanding.

● **Graphics software:** Graphics software is an application used to create and edit images. Graphics software has functions (e.g. drawing tools) that allow the user to create images. It also has a set of colour correction functions that allow the user to edit existing photographic images.

● **Types of image:** There are two types of image file: bitmap and vector. A bitmap takes an image and breaks it down into a grid of pixels. Each pixel is a single colour and the tiny squares of colour are used to make up detailed images. A vector image file contains instructions that the computer uses to redraw the image. For example, a single vector instruction might be 'draw a 4 centimetre line at 45 degrees'.

## ⏻ How to...

In the second part of the lesson students complete an exercise under your guidance.

In your introduction to this part of the lesson demonstrate how to access Google Docs through a browser. You don't need to go through the full set of Google Docs instructions. However, students need to open a blank image file and an existing photographic image during this part of the lesson and the activities that follow. Show the class how to open new and existing files. Point out where students can find the drawing tools menu and colour correction tools.

##  Now you do it...

Students open a new graphics file in Google Docs and create an image using the standard drawing tools available in the application. They choose a suitable file name and save the file.

**What success looks like:** Students navigate Google Docs with confidence and open a graphics file. They use a range of editing tools available in the graphics package. Using a new file name, students save the image they have created or modified.

## If you have time...

In this activity students extend their work, either:

- opening a new graphics file in Google Docs and creating an image using the standard drawing tools available in the application

or:

- opening an existing image using Google Docs and using the colour balance controls available in the software to change the image.

Whichever task each student chooses, the student thinks of a suitable name for the file and saves the file.

**What success looks like:** Students navigate Google Docs with confidence and open a graphics file. They use a range of editing tools available in the graphics package, building on their previous work. Using a new file name, students save the image they have created or modified.

##  Test yourself...

FOUNDATION QUESTIONS

**1**  What is a pixel? Answer: A pixel is a small square block that is a single colour. A pixel is the smallest element used to build up a bitmap image. The word 'pixel' stands for picture element.

**2**  Name two common features of graphics software. Answer: Correct responses include: colour correction; drawing; rotation; crop; scale.

EXTENSION QUESTIONS

**3**  Explain the difference between a vector and bitmap image. Answer: A bitmap image is made up of a grid of small squares of colour called pixels. A vector image is stored as a set of mathematical instructions that allow the computer to redraw the image as a set of lines and shapes.

**4**  What is the difference between contrast and brightening? Answer: In a graphics application, increasing the contrast creates a bigger difference between light and dark areas of the image. That is, it makes the light areas lighter and the dark areas darker. Increasing the brightness of an image makes all areas of the image lighter.

# 6.4 Creating a report

## Learning outcomes

When they have completed this lesson students should be able to:

- ↗ create a report using a template
- ↗ share a document online
- ↗ edit a document online
- ↗ add comments to documents online.

More-confident students will:

- ↗ add images to a document.

## Overview

In this lesson students use a collaborative online tool to create and share a document. Students work as part of a team. They use a template to create a report on an aspect of 'The impact of information technology on daily life'. Each student shares his or her work with other team members and team members add comments to one another's work. Students who add images to their report ensure that they appropriately credit the work they use.

## Language development

The original use of the word 'template' was in manufacturing and engineering. A template in engineering is a pattern or design that is made in rigid material, such as a thin sheet of metal. The template is used as a guide when cutting or drilling a component for an engine or other manufactured product. Templates are used in engineering to ensure that a component is the same every time it is manufactured.

In computing, a template is a pattern or design that is used as a guide when creating documents such as reports or newsletters. A presentation template ensures that every slide in a presentation looks the same.

## Before the lesson

Students work in teams to complete this lesson. Select the teams before the lesson begins. You should aim for a range of ability in each team. Where possible, ensure that there is a good spread of language ability in the groups. If you have students who need support with English, make sure there is someone confident with the English language in the same group. Identify team leaders. The members of a team should agree to use the same template.

Someone in the team will need to take the lead on that decision. The team members will also need to make sure they choose different aspects of the impact of information technology on daily life.

Try out a few searches to identify materials suitable as research pages, so that you are prepared to support students. Try search strings such as 'impact of computers on employment' or 'how computers have changed learning'.

The key words for this lesson are: comment boxes and template. The words are highlighted in the text the first time they appear. Their definitions are included in the Key words box at the end of the lesson. You may want to review these words before the lesson.

## ⌘ Learn about...

You will lead the first part of the lesson. Make sure students understand these ideas. You may ask them to make notes. You may use directed questioning to check understanding.

- **The structure of a report:** The structure of a basic report is a heading, introduction, body and conclusion. Students should present the report they create in the **'Now you do it...'** activity in this format.

- **Comment boxes:** Collaborative working allows members of a team to comment on each other's work. Comment boxes allow suggestions to be left for the author without affecting the main text.

- **Templates:** These provide a structure and format for a document. Templates ensure consistency and allow the author to concentrate on content without worrying too much about format. Students in each team should all use the same template.

## How to...

In the second part of the lesson students complete an exercise under your guidance.

Introduce templates and comments to students in this part of the lesson. Create a short document using a template. Ask one of your trusted students to log on and share the document with that student. Ask that student to add a comment so that other students can see how the process works.

Describe the '**Now you do it...**' activity to students. Explain that they will work in teams with all team members using the same template and sharing documents for comment.

## Now you do it...

Students work in a team to produce a report on how information technology has had an impact on daily life. Each team member chooses one aspect of of daily life from this list: the workplace, finance, education, entertainment, healthcare, shopping. The team chooses a standard report template from Google Apps. A student shares his or her document with all other students in the team. Team members comment on each other's contributions.

**What success looks like:** Students research the aspect of daily life they have chosen and identify at least three ways in which computers have changed the way we do things. Students' reports include a heading, introduction, body and conclusion. Students share their report with other team members and post at least one comment on each team member's report. Ideally, a comment should be constructive and suggest an improvement or correct an error.

## If you have time...

Students add an image to their completed report.

**What success looks like:** Students have identified an image that is relevant to the topic of their report. They demonstrate that they have permission to use the image and add any credits required to their report.

## Test yourself...

### FOUNDATION QUESTIONS

**1** List the four main report sections in order. Answer: The four main sections of a report are title, introduction, body and conclusion.

**2** Give an advantage of collaborative software. Answer: There are several possible answers including: collaborative software allows several people to share in the creation of a document; using collaborative software means documents don't have to be emailed to several people.

### EXTENSION QUESTIONS

**3** Discuss the advantages of using a template over using a blank document to create a report. Answer: The advantages of a template include: it makes the task of laying out the report easier; it means every report looks the same, so people reading it know what to expect; everyone in an organisation can use the same template, so there is consistency; a template can make a document look professional.

**4** Why is it useful to add comments to a document? Answer: Comments can be used to provide useful feedback to the person who wrote the document. They can be used to suggest changes or point out errors in the text.

# 6.5 Creating a slideshow presentation

pages 164–167

## Learning outcomes

When they have completed this lesson students should be able to:

↗ create a simple slideshow from a template

↗ create a slideshow from their own design.

More-confident students will:

↗ add a video file to a presentation slide.

## Overview

In this lesson students work collaboratively as part of a team to create a presentation on the impact of technology on daily life. Students use a range of functions in a presentation package to create an effective and consistent presentation. A team of students uses online collaborative tools to support group work.

## Before the lesson

In this lesson students will use Google Slides, the presentation software element of Google Docs. There are other presentation packages available and it may be that students are already familiar with an alternative, such as Microsoft PowerPoint. It is important that students use Google Slides in this lesson. Google Docs is used throughout this chapter to demonstrate how collaborative tools work.

Check that Google Slides can be accessed in a browser from a student's account before the lesson starts. Work through the demonstration in the 'How to...' part of this lesson. If students are familiar with another presentation package, make a note of similarities and differences between that application and Google Slides.

The key words for this lesson are presentation software. The words are highlighted in the text the first time they appear. Their definitions are included in the Key words box at the end of the lesson. You may want to review these words before the lesson.

## ⌘ Learn about...

You will lead the first part of the lesson. Make sure students understand these ideas. You may ask them to make notes. You may use directed questioning to check understanding.

- **Presentation software:** This is a software application that supports the creation of a slideshow. A slideshow can illustrate a presentation or lesson. The presenter can simply click to advance the slides. Presentations can also be run automatically to present information in public spaces, such as the entrance foyer of a building.

- **Common features of presentation packages:** There are many presentation packages available. They offer a set of common features including: themes, templates, master slides, animations, transitions, speaker notes and multimedia.

## ⏻ How to...

In the second part of the lesson students complete an exercise under your guidance. In your introduction to this part of the lesson show students how to access Google Slides. Show them how to locate the main menu and slide menu. Briefly demonstrate how students can:

- open a new file
- edit the master slide
- add new slides to a presentation
- add text and images
- add transitions and animations to a slide.

If students already have experience of using alternative presentation software (e.g. Microsoft PowerPoint) point out any similarities and differences. Involve students by using a session of questions and answers to check their understanding.

##  Now you do it...

Students stay in the same group they were in for the 'Now you do it...' activity in Lesson 6.4. Each student in the group creates presentation slides using the content that student researched in Lesson 6.4 on the impact of technology on daily life. As a group, students put all their slides together into a single presentation. They have to work collaboratively to: create and share a template for their group presentation; use an agreed template to create their slides; agree transitions; bring together individual contributions into a single slideshow and present the group slideshow. In your introduction to the activity make sure students understand the process. Appoint a team leader to coordinate the tasks.

**What success looks like:** Each student creates one or two slides summarising his or her contribution to the presentation. Students use the template and transitions agreed by the group. Every student contributes, including creating a template and putting together a single presentation from individual contributions. All team members contribute to the presentation of the slides to the class.

##  If you have time...

Students research the Internet to find a video that is relevant to their contribution to the presentation. If you feel it is necessary, advise students not to select a video that is too long—a video of no more than 30 seconds would be suitable. Students add the video to a presentation slide.

**What success looks like:** Students find a relevant video slide as a result of their Internet search. The video clip is appropriate in content and not too long. Students successfully insert the video into a slide. The slide need not be included in the group presentation.

##  Test yourself...

FOUNDATION QUESTIONS

**1** What is the difference between an animation and a transition? Answer: An animation applies an effect to an element of a presentation slide. This might be a piece of text or an image, for example. A transition is an effect that applies to a whole slide.

**2** Give two examples of presentation software. Answers include: Google Slides, Prezi, Microsoft PowerPoint, Impress.

EXTENSION QUESTIONS

**3** Explain the difference between a template and a theme. Answer: A template gives instructions for layouts, structures and themes for every part of a presentation. A theme gives instructions for colours, fonts and other styles.

**4** Name and explain four common features of presentation software. Answer:
   ○ **Master slide:** This lets the user set styles, colours, background and images that appear on every slide in the presentation.
   ○ **Transition:** Transitions set the way one slide changes to the next. They can include special effects, such as having the screen fade to black between slides.
   ○ **Animations:** These are effects used within a slide. For example, words and images can be moved around to add interest.
   ○ **Templates:** A template is a combination of layouts, structures and themes. Adding a template to your presentation will automatically change layouts, colours, backgrounds and fonts.

# 6.6 Creating a survey

## Learning outcomes

When they have completed this lesson students should be able to:

↗ understand peer assessment

↗ understand self-assessment

↗ explain the difference between quantitative and qualitative data

↗ create an online form.

More-confident students will:

↗ use self-assessment and peer-assessment questionnaires to reflect on the success of a piece of work.

## Overview

In this lesson students use survey software to create an online survey to evaluate a piece of their own work. Students will distribute the survey to a group of peers to be completed. Once the survey is closed a student will analyse and report on the results.

## Before the lesson

In this lesson students use Google Forms, the element of Google Docs that supports the creation of forms, questionnaires and other surveys. There are other packages available that perform similar functions but it is important that students use Google Forms in this lesson. Google Docs is used throughout this chapter to demonstrate how collaborative tools work.

Check that Google Forms can be accessed in a browser from a student's account before the lesson starts. Work through the demonstration in the '**How to…**' part of this lesson. It is unlikely that students have used similar software before, so prepare well in order to deliver a strong introduction.

The key words for this lesson are: peer assessment and self-assessment. The words are highlighted in the text the first time they appear. Their definitions are included in the Key words box at the end of the lesson. You may want to review these words before the lesson.

## ⌘ Learn about…

You will lead the first part of the lesson. Make sure students understand these ideas. You may ask them to make notes. You may use directed questioning to check understanding.

- **Quantitative data:** These are numeric data that are easy to measure or count. Quantitative data can be totalled, averaged and processed in other ways that allow comparisons to be made. Quantitative data measure something.

- **Qualitative data:** These are descriptive data that are usually in the form of words, not numbers. Qualitative data describe something.

- **Peer assessment:** An assessment carried out by a student's peers is known as peer assessment. Peers might be other members of a team or a wider group of people who have a similar outlook and background.

- **Self-assessment:** This is an assessment by an individual of his or her own actions or work.

## ⏻ How to…

In the second part of the lesson students complete an exercise under your guidance. Few students will have previous experience of forms software. A strong introduction to this part of the lesson will be key to success in the '**Now you do it…**' activity. In your introduction demonstrate how to:

- access the Google Forms software and open a new file

- create a new question

- send a survey to peers

- review the results of a survey.

You can help students by spending some time suggesting how to create questions that return measurable quantitative data. For example, suggest students ask those completing the survey to grade questions against a five-mark scale, rather than using open questions.

##  Now you do it...

Students use online questionnaire software (Google Forms) to gather feedback on the presentation they created in the Lesson 6.5 '**Now you do it...**' activity. Students create a questionnaire that includes a mix of qualitative and quantitative questions to use as a survey. They send the questionnaire to peers and gather feedback. Students review the survey results and write the findings.

**What success looks like:** Students create a well-structured questionnaire that includes a mix of clear qualitative and quantitative questions. Students send the questionnaire to a number of their peers with a deadline for completion. Students review the survey results and write clear and concise findings. The findings should include suggestions for improvements in future presentations.

##  If you have time...

Students create an online questionnaire that can be used for self-assessment of the presentation created in the Lesson 6.5 '**Now you do it...**' activity.

**What success looks like:** Students create and complete a self-assessment questionnaire. They draw on the questions used for peer assessment, but add questions that are appropriate for self-assessment. They may, for example, include a question about the way they approached the research, which would not be relevant to the peer group. Students add the findings to the review they have created.

##  Test yourself...

FOUNDATION QUESTIONS

**1** Explain the difference between qualitative and quantitative data. Answer: Quantitative data are data that can be measured numerically. Qualitative data are described in words.

**2** What is the difference between a check box and a dropdown box? Answer: A check box can only be ticked or unticked, and you may need several checkboxes for a range of answers. A dropdown box can have multiple text-based answers to choose from with only one action needed.

EXTENSION QUESTIONS

**3** Write three qualitative questions you could use to assess the quality of a slideshow. Answer: Examples of qualitative questions are: What type of multimedia would you have chosen to use instead of what was used? What did you like about the template? What did you think of the colours used?

**4** What are the limitations of asking qualitative questions? Answer: Qualitative questions cannot be measured numerically. That makes it difficult to compare the results of two questions. For example, if we have quantitative data we can say, 'The survey shows that 75 per cent of teachers think the presentation is well designed compared with only 45 per cent of students'. That kind of comparison cannot be made if we have qualitative data.

The test questions and assessment activities give you an opportunity to evaluate students' understanding. The questions are shown here with possible answers.

##  Model answers to test questions

1  Explain three ways in which technology has changed entertainment. Answer: Entertainment is now available 'on demand'. Previously, entertainment was scheduled at particular times. Technology means that entertainment can be interactive. In the past, entertainment (e.g. video and music) was purchased in shops. Today entertainment can be downloaded or streamed from any location.

2  Explain the difference between copyright and plagiarism. Answer: Copyright is the legal protection of intellectual property. Plagiarism takes place when someone uses another person's intellectual property and claims it as his or her own.

3  What is software piracy? Answer: Software piracy is the illegal copying and distribution of software, such as computer games.

4  What is an advantage of peer assessment? Answer: You receive a wide range of views and new ideas through peer assessment.

5  What questions would you ask yourself during self-assessment of your work? Answer: Examples are: Does my work meet the needs of the target audience? Is the design clear?

6  Explain what quantitative data are and give an example. Answer: Quantitative data can be measured and counted. An example is '85 per cent of website users approve of the background colour'.

7  What is a disadvantage of using qualitative questions when doing a survey? Answer: The results cannot be measured.

8  What is the difference between an animation and a transition? An animation applies an effect to an element of a presentation slide. This might be a piece of text or an image, for example. A transition is an effect that applies to a whole slide.

9  What is an advantage of using a theme when creating a slideshow? Answer: A theme can apply a professional look to a presentation in seconds.

10  What is collaborative technology? Answer: Collaborative technology uses a combination of hardware and software to help people work together, even if they are in remote locations.

##  Model answers to assessment activities

### Starter activity

All students should be able to complete this activity. Students open a Google Docs document and write a report on the difference between bitmap and vector graphics.

**What success looks like:** Students create a report on the difference between bitmap and vector graphics. Students:

- use a clear report structure with a title, introduction, body and conclusion
- show some evidence of research, referencing any text or images used from other sources.

### Intermediate activity

In this activity students create an image using the drawing tools in Google Drawings. The image is saved as a bitmap file and incorporated into the report created in the starter activity.

**What success looks like:** Students use the appropriate tools in Google Docs with confidence. They create an image and incorporate it into an existing report document. The image is relevant to the subject matter of the report. Students save the image as a bitmap (.bmp) file.

## Extension activity

Students work with a partner or in a small team. They share their work with each other. Each student reviews another's work and adds comments to the shared report, as appropriate.

**What success looks like:** Students successfully share the report they have created in the starter and intermediate activities. Each student accesses the shared file of a friend and opens it. Students identify a small number, perhaps three to five, areas for comment. They add clear concise notes to the text before saving it to be reviewed by its originator. The originator of the document reviews the friend's comments and makes appropriate changes to the report.